Sunset MEXICAN COOK BOOK

By the Editors of Sunset Books
and Sunset Magazine

922 -

922-9609 -Carol

Lane Books · Menlo Park, California

Mexican Cooking Made Easy

Cooking unfamiliar foreign food can be easy and fun only if you have the proper kind of recipes and help. This book will give that kind of guidance.

Often foreign cook books omit essential steps or make unsatisfactory ingredient substitutions. Not so here. Every recipe is complete and thoroughly tested. You do not have to read between the lines to have successful results.

Most of the dishes may be made with easily obtainable ingredients. In cases where special foods are required, the recipe often will give pertinent facts. Or you may consult the shopping guide in Chapter I to learn what the ingredients look like and where you may buy them.

Another troublesome aspect of making dishes from a foreign country may be the unfamiliar cooking techniques required. In this book you will find detailed instructions about methods which may be new to you, from such simple tasks as heating tortillas you buy to more complicated preparation, such as making tortillas from scratch. Often how-to-do-it photographs are an additional aid.

Edited by Marjorie Ray Piper

Special Consultant: Jerry Anne DiVecchio

ILLUSTRATIONS by Earl Thollander.

COVER PHOTOGRAPH by Glenn Christiansen. Dishes featured: on plate, Tacos (recipe on page 30) and Flautas (33); in bowl, Tomato Gazpacho with Avocado (69); in pitcher, Orange Sangría (94).

PHOTOGRAPHERS: Clyde Childress (page 83); Martin Litton (7); Ells Marugg (94); Darrow M. Watt (23, 26, 31, 38, 41, 46, 49, 50, 54, 60, 67, 70, 75, 86, 87, and 90); courtesy Western Growers Association (14); Baron Wolman Photography (11).

SPANISH LANGUAGE CONSULTANT, George Morrill.

Executive Editor, Sunset Books: David E. Clark

Fourteenth Printing May 1974

CONTENTS

A TOUR OF MEXICAN FOODS

Shopping and dining South of the Border or in the U.S.

When the Spanish ambassadors of Cortez first visited the court of the Aztec emperor Moctezuma in 1519, they were greeted with lavish gifts of precious metals and banquets of exquisite concoctions new to them. Who is to say whether the Spaniards lusted more for the gold or the good dinners of that land which is now Mexico?

Historians may weigh the pros and cons of their conquest, but epicureans know the results were favorable. The food of Mexico today—a blend of Indian, Spanish, and other acquisitive or peaceful cultures—preserves the virtues of all. The resulting cuisine is a delight of contrasts— colorful and earthy, exciting and soothing, primitive and polished. At times it is regal and refined, other times robust and brassy as a mariachi band.

FOOD SPICED WITH HISTORY

Just as the traditional American Thanksgiving foods bring to mind images from the past, Mexican foods elicit their own historical tableaus when you know something of their origin.

The Indians, both Mayan and Aztec, cultivated corn, beans, and chiles hundreds of years before the Spanish came. Many familiar dishes, such as Tamales, were being made then.

The Spaniards were naturally intrigued by the many foods grown by the Aztecs, who were highly advanced in horticulture. Among these were foods now important to the modern world: tomatoes, avocados, sweet and white potatoes, peanuts, squash, pineapple, papayas, and vanilla A few kinds of beans and chiles were already known in the Orient, and broad beans were grown in the Mediterranean area, but those in Mexico were all new to the Spanish.

The ships that returned to Europe were laden with seeds and cuttings, which flourished in various climates. Some of the foods were quickly accepted and others, such as the tomato, were resisted as poisonous for a time. But now all these things are grown throughout the world.

Another strange food which particularly attracted the Spanish was mixed with water to make a beverage—chocolate. Cocoa had special significance to the Aztecs. The beans were used as currency. The drink had royal and religious status—only men of high rank were allowed to sip it. Chocolate became popular throughout Europe after the Spanish discovered that sugar made the sour Aztec potion much more palatable and delicious.

The Spaniards also introduced many new foods and methods of preparation to Mexico. They brought boatloads of cattle, sheep, chickens, wheat, rice, nuts, spices such as cinnamon and cloves, and fruits such as peaches and apricots. Many of these foods were the just desserts of conquest in reverse. Centuries before, the Spanish had gained these from the Moors who had conquered them.

The Spanish also introduced the use of oil and wine in cooking. Their nuns were in good part responsible for spreading the knowledge of how to use their foods among native women. Because cooking was an art that could be enjoyed within the confines of religious practice, the nuns became famous for their culinary creations. They developed many new dishes by combining the ingredients they knew with those the Indians grew and used.

Later other European countries influenced the diet. French, Austrian, and Italian dishes were introduced through the court of Maximilian of Hapsburg, whom Napoleon III tried to establish as ruler of Mexico in the 1860's.

Over the years, the cuisine has been influenced by immigrants from many countries, by foreign travel, and by the mass media. But whatever Mexico has adopted from other countries usually has a distinctly Mexican character.

STAFFS OF LIFE

Although many new foods and ways of preparing them have been introduced over the centuries, the corn, beans, and chiles grown by the Aztecs are still the staffs of Mexican life.

Corn was so important to the Indians that they built temples and held festivals to honor Centeotl, goddess of earth and maize. Today most Mexicans are as dependent on corn as Orientals are on rice. The fresh grain is used in a variety of dishes. Ground dried corn (*masa*) is the basis for breads, numerous prepared dishes, and a beverage, Atole. Even the husks are used, as wrappers for Tamales.

Corn masa is so important to Mexican cooking that two chapters of this book are devoted to cooking with it. The Tortilla and Tamale chapters tell how to buy the product and how to prepare some of the best-known and best-loved dishes.

Beans may be served in some form at every meal. A bubbling pot of them is omnipresent in the Mexican kitchen. They are served where potatoes would be in the United States. Mashed as Refried Beans (Frijoles Refritos), they not only are served as a starchy accompaniment but also are treated as a sauce, to fill or top many dishes.

Many kinds of beans are used in a spectrum of colors—white, yellow, pink, red, maroon, brown, and black.

Chiles are probably the ingredient that spells "Mexican food" to foreigners everywhere. Dozens of varieties, both mild and hot, are grown. The mild, sweet ones—some of which are also a bit peppery—comprise a main part of appetizer, entrée, snack, or vegetable dishes. Hot

chiles are an integral part of a few dishes, but generally are added for seasoning. Pickled mild or hot chiles may be a relish or garnish. Many sauces contain chopped chiles or pulp; a few even contain the seeds, toasted and crushed.

THE MEXICAN MARKETPLACE

In the bustling open-air markets so prevalent even in a modern Mexico, fresh produce is heaped high in a mad, colorful, aromatic array.

Many fruits, vegetables, and herbs are familiar to the American *turista*. But others are strange, lending the note of exotica sightseers expect.

Among the well-known vegetables, in addition to those the Indians originated already mentioned, may be tiny orange carrots, spinach, chard, lettuces, beets, artichokes, celery, watercress, parsley, and both sweet and white potatoes.

Recognizable fruits are oranges, grapefruit, tangerines, pomegranates, and limes, which are called *limones* and are much more used than lemons.

Other fruits may be familiar, but of unfamiliar variety. Papayas are large like melons, with flesh that ranges from pale yellow to brilliant orange and even pink. The pineapples are gigantic. Bananas are both yellow and red, in a variety of sizes. Mangoes may also be of various sizes and colors, including yellow, red, or purple. Some of the tropical fruits, such as guavas and passion fruit, may be recognizable only to Americans from certain parts of the West or Hawaii. All the temperate-zone fruits and melons are sold in variety, too.

Some of the exotic vegetables there are now occasionally seen in American markets, such as the papaya-shaped, apple-green *chayote* squash or the large gray-brown root, *jícama*.

Others are almost completely unknown—the sweet *huacamotes*, a kind of yucca which is eaten cooked, and *nopales*, the leaves of prickly pear cactus with taste and texture something like green beans when sliced into *nopalitos*. Squash blossoms (*flores de calabaza*) displayed are not for arranging in vases but for cooking as a vegetable or garnishing dishes.

Some of the leafy vegetables are strange, such as *verdolagas* (the common garden weed, purslane) and *romeritas* (resembling rosemary).

Unusual fruits also abound. The heart-shaped, spiny soursop, which has the much more musical name *guanábana*, makes excellent conserve and juice. The *chirimoya* is a relative of the soursop but is sweeter (some people say it tastes like vanilla ice cream); it is eaten raw and used in desserts.

Cactus (*tuna*) is one of the most curious fruits, ranging from green to red to maroon. The moist, granular flesh inside the spiny oval pod is good raw with lemon and sugar, but also is candied or used in salads and drinks.

Sapote, granadilla, and *mamey* are names of other unusual fruits sold.

Other curiosities in the market place are bunches of herbs, various dried plants used to make tea or other drinks, and pumpkin and melon seeds to nibble or to crush for making beverages and sauces.

THE MOBILE MARKETS

The markets are not the only places for shopping or snacking. Vendors set up sidewalk booths to sell produce, make Tacos on the spot over small charcoal braziers, or offer more simple treats such as slices of raw jícama or oranges to dip in chile powder. Some sell whole coconuts with straws inserted through the punctured "eyes" for sipping the milk (don't try to walk away with the shell—the vendor expects to get it back).

Some stands have glass barrels filled with fruitades in a rainbow of colors and flavors.

Not all of the vendors are stationary. Some move around. The sweets peddlers may carry trays of candy, including candied fruits and vegetables, or Flan (caramel custard). The bakery boy travels on bicycle with a basket of fresh bread balanced on his head.

Goat milk is sold on the hoof. The vendor leads a nanny goat through the streets and milks it to order.

Other vendors, those of fruits and vegetables, may lead a laden donkey or push a wooden cart.

In the cities now, not all of the cart-pushers are vendors. Some are shoppers pushing through the maze of a *super mercado*, that American institution the supermarket.

BRASEROS & BLENDERS

The next step from the market place is into the kitchen.

In country areas or poorer homes, some kitchens are still much like the primitive ones of centuries ago. The clay brazier called a *brasero*, or even several large stones, may serve as a stove. The beans may be cooked in an earthenware *olla*, a deep pot, or a stew in the earthenware *cazuela*, a wide casserole.

The hot chocolate drink will be beaten to a froth with the wooden *molinillo* devised by ancient Indians and perhaps poured from a clay pitcher or *jarro*.

The old-fashioned cook will still grind her own corn to make masa, using the pitted-stone, oblong mortar called a *metate* and the stone pestle called a *metlapil*. She will pat tortillas into shape with her hands and bake them on a flat, unglazed earthenware or iron griddle called a *comal*. To grind chiles, herbs, nuts, and chocolate, she may use a smaller, three-legged mortar of stone called *molcajete* with its matching pestle, the *tejolote*.

Some of these primitive utensils are still functional in the most ultra-modern apartments of Mexico City. Amidst the electric range and metal cooking equipment may be ollas, a molinillo, and a brasero still in use. The cook may place an old-style comal on the electric burner for cooking tortillas; but probably she flattened them into shape with a tortilla press and undoubtedly she bought commercially ground masa.

The stone mortars and pestles are probably the only utensils falling into relative disuse in the modern kitchen. They are victims of the faster food mills and electric blenders.

COMIDAS & COFFEE BREAKS

Just as Mexicans use both the old and new in foods, as well as methods and utensils for preparation, they also enjoy dining in ways both traditional and modern.

The customary meals and times for eating them developed out of the work schedule of a rural people, with some consideration of Spanish habits. It's no surprise, therefore, that the old ways are still more closely followed in the country and changes have taken place in the cities to suit the demands of business life.

In the country, breakfast (*desayuno*) is a light meal shortly after the cock crows, enough to tide a person over while doing early chores. Later in the morning a breakfast (*almuerzo*) of fortifying foods is eaten, undoubtedly to give energy for heavy work.

As in most farm areas throughout the world, the big meal of the day is the midday one. In Mexico, this *comida* generally begins about 2 p.m. The multi-course lunch may go on several hours and be followed by a siesta. The later hour and siesta, of course, are Spanish-influenced customs, well-suited to areas where it is wise to rest during the heat of the day.

Very late in the afternoon or early evening, a snack or light supper called the *merienda* is eaten. A real supper called *cena* is served at home long after the sun has set. A late meal in a restaurant may be called a comida if it qualifies as the main meal of the day. The custom of eating into the wee hours is also Spanish.

Today in the cities, the pattern has changed some. Office workers may take almuerzo as a coffee break or, if they have missed breakfast, a sort of a fashionable brunch. Their comida may be much lighter, without a siesta following because some businesses no longer close for one. The merienda is becoming any kind of light meal eaten in the evening.

A lot of feeling still exists that it isn't healthful to eat much at night, particularly in places like Mexico City where the altitude is great—perhaps a very wise assumption. But more and more people are having larger meals then, often at restaurants or at dinner parties.

The large cities are sophisticated places, with numerous Continental and other foreign restaurants which serve past midnight. Many people live much according to the same patterns which

MERCADO LIBERTAD in Guadalajara is a bustling market of open stalls heaped with strange and familiar foods.

have become almost international in urban centers everywhere.

Nevertheless, customs do not change radically overnight anywhere. The main meal is still the comida. And the meal times are definitely later than they are in North America.

Visitors have found it wise to dine an hour or more later than they ordinarily would. Restaurants may not open for breakfast before 9 a.m. People used to eating earlier may have to go to a street booth for fruit juice or a snack such as a Taco or Empanada (meat or fruit-filled turnover) —foods such as these are eaten any time of day.

Anyone who goes to lunch even at 1 p.m. will find the good tables empty and have time to order before the place begins filling with local customers. Dinner likewise begins late, about 8 p.m. and on to midnight.

The kinds of dishes served at the various meals, of course, vary tremendously. But there are some traditional types. Desayuno, a "Continental" breakfast, usually is just sweet rolls and hot chocolate or Café con Leche (coffee with milk). Almuerzo might be composed of hearty breakfast sorts of things—eggs, meat, tortillas, beans, and fruit or fruit juice. Or it could consist of *antojos* (Tacos, Tostadas, and Enchiladas) or a plain broiled steak.

Comida for special occasions, or in the home of someone who lives more in the old manner, can be a gigantic, multi-coursed feast. First comes an appetizer, then a soup, and then a Sopa Seca or "dry soup"—really more like the pilaf or pasta courses in other countries. Then fish, meat (with salad or vegetable), and bean courses follow. A rich dessert or fruit may end the meal. Beverages served might be beer, wine, coffee, tea, fruit juice, or *pulque* (the fermented juice of the agave or century plant, comparable to beer in alcoholic content, usually only served in poorer homes).

Coffee or tea is always served after the dessert. Tortillas or *bolillos* (hard rolls) and a chile sauce are on the table throughout the meal.

Comida on a smaller scale, for either a person not too well off or even a señorita who is watching her calories, could be simply a stew, beans, and tortillas.

Those who take merienda as a "tea time" would have nothing but hot chocolate and rolls. Others who make it their only evening meal (like English high tea) could perhaps add antojos, beans, tortillas, or any of the dishes that would be served for lunch or breakfast.

Snacking naturally takes place at any time. American soft drinks are available everywhere, as in most countries of the globe, but fruit juices are also downed in quantity along with the numerous filling tidbits available.

THE TURISTA GOURMET

The foreign visitor should be prepared for surprises whenever or wherever he eats. There are many regional and seasonal specialties, as well as differences in customs from place to place.

Hotels and restaurants often gear their menus to the tastes of tourists. Some offer few typical dishes. Others may specialize in foods of European countries.

Many cafes and restaurants are a delight. They may be nothing more than plain board tables with straight wooden chairs set under a tree or beside the sea. Or they may be posh establishments replete with glorious tiles, wrought ironwork, waterfalls and pools, and lush tropical foliage. The open-air restaurants and sidewalk cafes are very pleasant places to enjoy the weather or watch the people.

Of course, some of the eateries are nothing but eateries. And some are plain and neat, or plain and suspect.

The traveler who loves to try new dishes will find that many of the typical foods are much different from those served in American Mexican restaurants.

The lucky gourmet will find a place to sample suckling pig or spit-roasted kid, pigeons and game birds, or seafoods. Two worth trying are squid and *langostinos,* a type of crayfish. If especially lucky, he will arrange to be invited to a barbecue, where a whole lamb or kid may be cooked in a pit lined with leaves of the agave (a succulent also used for brewing alcoholic *pulque* and *tequila*). The Mexican barbecue is much like an Hawaiian luau.

The traveler with a sense of humor and some knowledge of Spanish will have a field day trying all the dishes with funny names. With luck this person may succeed in trying some Tablecloth Stainers, Lady-Sized Mouthful, Old Clothes, Rooster's Beak, Chicken in Trousers, and even Chicken in the Garden. If he has a penchant for dishes made with spirits, he may enjoy Drunken Chicken, Drunken Turtledoves, Drunken Cupcakes, and the Drunken Sauce served at barbecues. Mexicans love to make jokes with recipe names.

The tourist with no gourmet inclinations can enjoy the country most merely by eating a lot of food, particularly when visiting in someone's home. A small appetite may be construed as a sign of unfriendliness.

Dining adventures await any foreigner. For Mexico is a large place of many climates. The people have diverse background, education, and tastes. The country is both very old and ultramodern, untouched and sophisticated. It definitely is a place for adventure, culinary and otherwise.

SHOPPING "BACK IN THE U.S."

A surprising number of the ingredients sold in Mexico are available now in the United States. If you live in one of the states near Mexico or in a large city, you will probably be able to find nearly everything called for in the small percentage of recipes which require special ingredients (most of the recipes in this book don't).

It may require a bit of detective work to track down more unusual items. Gourmet food departments in large supermarkets, department stores, and delicatessens are good places to search. Supermarkets near universities with many foreign students or in areas where minority groups tend to live are the best possibilities. Telephone ahead to check whether a certain item is stocked; if a store does not carry it, the clerk may be able to tell you who does. Shopping can be simplified if you let your fingers do all the walking.

You may have to snoop around once you get to a store, too. Mexican products are not always displayed in one spot. Tortillas may be with the frozen foods, canned green chiles near the olives and pickles, and the red chile sauce beside the tomato paste. Again, some question-asking will save time. Ask the manager where you might find what you want. If he does not stock it, he may order it if you let him know there is a demand.

Perhaps the best way to locate Mexican foods is to ask someone who is Mexican where to shop. You may inquire at Mexican restaurants and even find that the owner will sell you what you want out of his supplies.

The availability of Mexican foods varies from very easy to find to impossible, depending on what the ingredient is and where you live. Here is a glossary of foods, keyed with letters, to help you know where a certain thing may be found. Exceptions exist to any rule, but in general the foods can be grouped according to availability as follows:

(A) At almost all markets

(B) At large supermarkets or smaller stores which stock a variety of the foreign foods most in demand

(C) Probably only at supermarkets with large foreign or gourmet departments, delicatessens or gourmet food shops, or Mexican groceries

(D) Probably only at Mexican groceries or markets in areas of large Mexican population

Achiote (Annatto). (D) Reddish-brown seeds which are boiled in water to make a substance for coloring rice and sauces a rich saffron yellow. A powdered form is known in the United States as butter coloring.

-Ates. (C and D) A suffix to words indicating sweet pastes of guava, quince, mango, or papaya. These make a good dessert with cheese and crackers.

Atole. (D) A gruel-like corn meal drink flavored with fruit or chocolate. Some Mexican markets now sell foil packets of instant Atole to which water or milk is added.

Azafrán. Saffron (A), sometimes Mexican saffron (D) from an entirely different plant than that which produces the expensive saffron from Europe or Asia generally sold by American spice companies.

Beans. Dried pink, red, pinto, and kidney beans are much used. (A) Dried black beans and garbanzos are a little more difficult to find. (B) Cooked red, kidney, pinto, garbanzo beans, and prepared Refried Beans come in cans. (A) Dried broad beans are less easily obtainable. (D)

Café. Coffee. Mexican blends may be purchased in cans. (C) Or American coffee can be brewed stronger than usual.

Cheese. Occasionally you can find imported Mexican cheeses. (D) But jack cheese (either the soft or hard-grating kind as the recipe specifies), Parmesan, Romano, and Cheddar make very good substitutes for various types. Longhorn Cheddar has melting qualities much like a cheese used in Mexico and therefore is recommended. (A)

Chiles. See pages 12 through 15 for detailed information about the various chiles and where to buy them. Most are very easy to find; just a few are obtainable only at Mexican stores.

Chocolate. (C) Cinnamon-flavored, sweetened Mexican chocolate is sold in cakes. See recipe for making hot chocolate drink on page 93. The Spanish word is also "chocolate."

Chorizo. (A and B) Highly seasoned link sausages. If these are not sold in your area, you can make them from the recipe on page 23.

Cilantro. (B and C) Fresh coriander leaves, which look much like ordinary parsley but have an entirely different flavor. This is the same herb as "Chinese parsley" sold in many Oriental markets. If you cannot buy it, you can grow your own from the coriander seed sold by many spice companies.

Cinnamon. Mexican stick cinnamon (D) is a little different in flavor from that usually sold in the United States. It also looks different—thin layers of bark are rolled up, rather than one thick piece of bark.

Enchilada Sauce. (A and B) The red sauce made of mild chile pulp used for Enchiladas is put up in cans by a number of companies. Or you can make your own by the Red Chile Sauce recipe on page 21 if you can obtain large dried *ancho, pasilla,* or California chiles. (D)

Epazote. (D) An herb much used in Mexico but rarely available in the United States. No recipes in this book require it.

Frijoles Refritos. Refried Beans, available in cans or made by recipe on page 22. (A)

Green Chile Salsa. (A and B) A relish-sauce of tomatoes, onions, and mild green chiles sold in cans or jars. You can also make a similar Fresh Tomato and Green Chile Sauce from the recipe on page 20.

Guanábana Nectar. (D) Canned fruit drink made from soursops, with flavor much like that of canned lichees or pears.

Guayabate. (C and D) Sweet, firm jam-like paste made from guavas, delicious for dessert served on slices of mild cheese, such as jack.

Harina. (A) Flour—regular all-purpose American wheat flour may be used. (Also see Masa listing.)

Jamaica. (D) This dark maroon dried flower is used to make a sweet, fruity beverage. The flowers are steeped in cold water for four hours or more to produce a cranberry-flavored, pink liquid, which is strained and sweetened to taste and served ice-cold.

Jícama. (C and D) This brownish-gray-skinned root vegetable has white, crisp meat resembling that of a potato. It tastes so much like fresh water chestnuts that Chinese cooks often use it as a substitute. Shaped something like a turnip, jícama grows to a foot or more in diameter. Some are sold whole, but very large ones may be cut in half or quarters. Just peel the thin skin away to use raw in the several recipes in this book calling for jícama. *See photo on next page.*

Lard. (A and B) Lard is much used as a deep-frying fat in Mexico and for making Tamale dough.

Manzanilla. (D) Dried flowers used to brew tea.

Masa and Masa Harina. (C and D) Fresh *masa* is a moist dough of ground *nixtamal* (dried corn which has been soaked in limewater and then cooked). When you can find it, usually only at certain Mexican stores or restaurants, buy only as much as you will use soon—it does not keep well.

A more widely used form of masa in the United States is a flour of dehydrated masa, sometimes also called corn tortilla or Tamale flour, or instant masa. You just add water to produce a dough very much like fresh masa.

A large part of the dehydrated masa flour sold in the United States is made by The Quaker Oats Company. The registered trademark name of their product is Masa Harina, further identified on packages by the generic term, "instant masa."

Mole. (C and D) Mole is a sauce used for meat and poultry, made with chiles, various spices, and sometimes chocolate. Often crushed sesame seed, pumpkin seed, or nuts are incorporated for flavor and thickening.

Powdered and paste bases for the sauce are sold in cans and jars. Follow label directions, adding meat stock or water, to make the sauce.

JÍCAMA, a large root vegetable delicious raw, now is sold at many U.S. markets featuring foreign foods.

CACTUS PADS, called Nopales, have a crisp, vegetable-like quality when peeled. They are also sold canned.

Nopales. (C and D) The leaves or pads of the prickly pear cactus are sometimes sold fresh and, more often, canned or in jars (called *nopalitos*). They can be used alone as a vegetable or in soups, salads, and omelets. *See photo above.*

Piloncillo. (D) Brown, unrefined cane sugar in small, hard, cone-shaped loaves used for sweetening coffee and desserts. It tastes something like molasses when dissolved in water. The sugar is sometimes sold in little bags (B and C) labelled by its other name, *panocha*.

Pine Nuts (Piñón). (A and B) Seeds of large pine cones with mild resinous flavor used as a nut. Be sure to buy them shelled—the tiny rice-grain-shaped nuts are very difficult to shell whole.

Pipián. (C and D) Sauce of chiles and spices (a variation of *mole*) thickened with seeds such as sesame or pumpkin. Available in powdered form canned or paste form bottled.

Red Chile Sauce. (A and B) Made from the pulp of large, mild, dried red chiles, this sauce used for preparing a variety of dishes is sold in cans of various sizes. You may also make it from the recipe on page 21. Throughout this book it is referred to as Mexican red chile sauce so that it will not be confused with the bottled tomato "chili" sauce resembling ketchup, an entirely different product.

Salsa Jalapeña. (A and B) This is a hot sauce-relish made of jalapeño chiles, onions, and tomatoes. It comes in two forms, one made with red tomatoes and the other made with green ones.

Taco Sauce. (A) Numerous canned and bottled sauces to use with Tacos are sold. These contain either red or green tomatoes, chiles for "heat," vinegar, onions, and seasonings.

Tomatillo or Tomate Verde. (C and D) This is a sweet green tomato about the size of a walnut (or smaller) with a parchment-like, gray-brown covering which looks something like dried leaves and is easily stripped away. The little tomato, very different in flavor from the green version of an ordinary tomato *(jitomate)*, is used in sauces. Plain canned ones, as well as several sauces made from them, are sold.

Tomato "Hot" Sauces. (A) A variety of peppery to very hot sauces of tomatoes and chiles are canned and bottled.

Tuna. (D) Cactus fruit good for dessert. Instructions for preparing are on page 89.

CHILES – SOME HOT, SOME NOT

If you conjured up a mental picture of a Mexican kitchen, undoubtedly you would include the hanging strings of dried red chiles called *ristras* amidst the painted tiles and clay cooking pots. For chiles probably typify Mexican cooking more than any one other food, unless it be corn or beans.

The widespread impression that Mexican cooks use chiles often is accurate. In fact, the varieties and ways they are used seem infinite. Perhaps the only misconception about chiles is that all are red-hot. Instead, many of the peppers are sweet, mild, or richly flavored at most.

The variety of chile names, kinds, and uses is probably the most fascinating aspect of Mexican cookery. Anyone who wants to know all about chiles should be a detective, research librarian, anthropologist, and botanist rolled into one.

However, you who merely want to cook some good and simple dishes can learn all you need to become an instant expert from the following pages. You will also read some unnecessary but interesting facts which will make your ventures into chile cooking much more fun.

THE MAD, MAD CHILE WORLD

A rose may be simply a rose, but a pepper can be either a chile or a chili or a chilli, depending on how you choose to spell it in English.

Throughout this book, "chile" is used because it is the same spelling name used by Mexicans in the Spanish language. But American manufacturers of spices and chile products usually label their products "chili." In England or the British Commonwealth countries, "chilli" is commonly used.

The word, however written, comes from the Nahuatl dialect of the Aztecs and was applied by the Spaniards to any kind of pepper of the chile family (this means that the expression "chile pepper" is redundant).

Chiles are all members of the genus *Capsicum*. This is an entirely different group of plants from those of the genus *Piper* which produces the berry that is ground to make black and white pepper. Ordinary bell peppers and pimientos are Capsicums and therefore also chiles.

Some historians say that all cultivated species originated on the American continent, while others insist a few kinds were known in Asia and elsewhere. Whatever the case, the chiles Columbus brought back to Europe from his first trip were new, an instant success, and soon grown all over the world.

Chiles of all varieties produce some kind of fleshy pod containing numerous seeds; this "pepper" is the fruit of the plant. Beyond this general description, little else can be said that will apply to all varieties. The peppers range in size from as small as a pea to more than a foot long. Some are very mild and sweet while others are so hot just touching them to the tongue is painful. Oddly enough, the larger the chile the milder the flavor usually is. The tiniest ones tend to pack the most wallop.

When the peppers are fresh and what growers call "immature," they may be green, yellow, white, or other colors. As they ripen on the vine, they change color to yellow, orange, red, or even chocolate brown. No matter what their color when fresh, they usually turn some shade of orange, red, or brown when dried.

Chile plants themselves do nothing to simplify the complex situation. They cross-pollinate freely. They even have the habit of producing both hot and mild peppers on the same plant at times.

Chiles grow in different shapes, too. Some are bulbous, oval, or heart-shaped; others are long and tapered, conical, or cylindrical. Still others are somewhat cubical or box-shaped as the bell pepper is.

Just as the peppers themselves are tremendously varied, so are the forms in which they are sold. Fresh ones may be bought either in their green, immature form or ripe and mature. Dried ones are sold whole, crumbled, or ground. Whole or sliced peppers also are canned (packed in water, oil, or sauce) or bottled (usually pickled).

Chile Sauces. Chiles also are incorporated in a variety of canned and bottled sauces. Among these are: Taco sauce (made with either red or green tomatoes); mild red chile sauce and the similar Enchilada sauce; green chile salsa (of mildly hot chiles, tomatoes, and onions); salsa jalapeña (of hot chiles and either red or green tomatoes); *mole* powder or paste (of many spices) to make a rich meat sauce; and various hot tomato sauces.

CHILES SOLD IN AMERICA

The following detailed information about chile powders and dried or fresh peppers will help you shop. You will know just what color, size, and shape each has, as well as how it is packaged.

Chile Powder and Paprika. The familiar American chile powder is a blend of ground dried chiles and other seasonings including cumin and oregano. In Mexican stores, powders of pure chile are sold, ranging from very mild and sweet to very hot.

Paprika is nothing but a powder of a mild, sweet chile.

Small Red Dried Hot Chiles. Many small, tapered chiles about 1 to 2 inches long are sold dried, but there is no one name to apply to all of them. The many varieties are imported from Japan or Africa, as well as Central or South America. Sometimes' Mexican stores will call any kind of these hot peppers *chiles de árbol*, but the true árbol is a specific variety which grows wild.

Among these are the *pulla* from Mexico, several inches long and very thin; the *hontaka* from Japan, which is shorter (often found in pickling spice mixtures); and the *sontaka*, also from Japan. These usually are not identified by name.

The smallest dried chiles, often no larger than a pea, are called *pequín* or *tepín (piquín* or *chiltepín)*, pronounced "peh-*keen*" or "teh-*peen.*" They are sold by many American spice companies. Usually the perfectly round ones are called tepín and little oval ones pequín. These little chiles are among the very hottest available.

Bell Peppers. The most familiar member of the *Capsicum* (chile) family is the bell pepper.

Like all chiles, bell peppers change color as they mature on the vine. The red bell peppers which appear in markets briefly in the fall are just mature versions of the green ones. Although they are a fiery color and therefore give the impression of having hotter flavor, red bells are really more sweet and mild.

Pimientos. The pimiento purchased canned in the United States is a heart-shaped chile. The flesh is slightly softer and a little more sweet than that of a red bell pepper.

California Green Chiles (Anaheim). This pepper is about 5 to 8 inches long and 1½ to 2 inches in diameter at the top, tapering to a point. Fresh ones are usually a bright, shiny green. When canned, they are soft and a moss green. Some mature ones which have turned red are sold both canned and fresh in the fall.

The flavor of California chiles ranges from mild and sweet like a bell pepper, to mildly hot. Whenever using either fresh or canned ones, taste for hotness.

These peppers are a variety cultivated principally in the United States and not often seen in Mexico, although very similar types called by several names are grown there.

Canned California green chiles are very easy to find at supermarkets in the West now, usually labeled just "Whole Chiles," "Diced Chiles," or "Green Chiles." Ask where they are displayed. They could be in the gourmet foods section, with pickles and olives, with a special Mexican foods section, or in some unexpected place. Be sure you do not get the can labeled "Hot Peppers," which contains very hot jalapeño chiles.

The canned chiles are very easy to use. Just rinse them, cut a slit in the side, and gently pull out the seeds and pith with your fingers. They are already peeled and partially cooked. The peeling process uses heat to blister off an unpleasant, somewhat tough skin; the process also gives a delightful roasted flavor.

Fresh bright-green California chiles are in most abundant supply through the summer and into early fall. To use these in cooking, it is wise to peel the skin from the chiles by the process described on the following page.

California or Anaheim (fresh)

California or Anaheim (dried)

Armenian Yellow Wax

Ancho (fresh)

Ancho (dried)

Ordinary Bell Pepper

Yellow Wax Chile

Fresno or Chile Verde

Caribe

Serrano

Floral Gem

Hontaka

Jalapeño

Pulla

Cascabel

How to Peel Fresh California Green Chiles. Wash chiles, wipe dry, and arrange on a broiler rack, close together. Preheat broiler unit and put rack underneath so that the top of the chiles is about 1 inch below the heat unit. Turn chiles frequently until blistered and lightly browned all over (but not limp). Watch closely. As each chile is done, drop it into a plastic bag.

When all are blistered, close bag and let stand until cool enough to handle (5 to 10 minutes). Remove one chile at a time, and peel by using a sharp paring knife to catch the skin and pull it gently away. Catch the skin wherever it appears loosest; the peel will come off in several uneven pieces. Be careful not to tear the chiles if you need to use them whole for stuffing; if a piece of peel refuses to come off easily, leave it on.

Then lay each chile flat and cut a lengthwise slit in one side to within about ¼ inch of the stemmed top. Carefully reach in with a spoon and remove all the seeds, white core, and pith. If you are going to make Chiles Rellenos, try to do this without weakening the stem end, which you may use as a handle for dipping the whole stuffed chiles into batter. For other uses, you may cut off the stem and hard top. Rinse out seeds.

You can peel chiles a day ahead of when you need to use them; just wrap in clear plastic wrap and refrigerate. Chiles freeze well, too, and keep as long as 9 months if at 0° or colder.

Note: Ordinary bell peppers can be peeled by this same method. See preceding page for description of California chiles.

Fresno Chiles. Like the California chile, this one also is primarily grown in the United States. Bright green when fresh and changing to orange and then red as it matures, the Fresno has a conical shape about 2 inches long and 1 inch in diameter at the stem end.

It is much hotter than the California chile, although it varies from mildly hot to painful. This pepper is usually pickled (not identified as a Fresno—just "Hot Peppers"). You can chop the fresh, raw pepper to add heat to sauces or salads.

Serrano Chiles. (Pronounced "seh-*rrrah*-noh") These little peppers are about 1 or 1½ inches long, ½ inch in diameter, and cylindrical. They are very, very hot.

When fresh, they are a rich, waxy green; they change to orange and then red as they mature.

Occasionally you will find fresh ones in markets, particularly those catering to Mexican trade. But usually serranos are sold canned, pickled, or packed in oil. Because they are so hot and are used only for zippy flavor, it may not matter which form you use in a recipe.

Jalapeño Chiles. (Pronounced "hah-la-*peh*-nyoh") The fresh pepper is a dark green, about 2½ inches long and about 1 inch in diameter at the stem end. It is very hot. Fresh ones are not often marketed, but various canned and pickled forms are readily available.

The canned peppers are sometimes labelled "Hot Peppers," with jalapeño as a subtitle. They are sold pickled in bottles, sometimes called "Hot Peppers" or labelled by their name. They are also available in a sauce, salsa jalapeña.

Mexican stores also carry canned *chipotle* peppers (sometimes spelled *chipocle* or *chilpotle*), which are just mature (red) jalapeños which have been smoked. However, none of the recipes in this book call for chipotles.

Ancho and Mulato Chiles. (Pronounced "*ahn*-choh" and "moo-*lah*-toh") The ancho looks very much like the ordinary bell pepper. It has much the same shape and flavor, although it can be considerably more peppery at times. But it differs in having a more firm, less crisp texture, a little darker green color, more waxy-looking skin, and more tapered rather than "square" shape. Like the bell pepper, it turns a bright, beautiful red in the fall, at the same time sweetening in flavor.

Much confusion exists concerning the ancho. Many Mexicans and merchants call them *pasillas* (as they likewise call pasillas by the name of anchos). But botanists identify the ancho as the one that resembles a bell pepper and the pasilla as a long, thin pepper. Both kinds may be called just "Mexican chiles."

When dried, anchos assume a flat, round shape about 3 or 4 inches in diameter and become very wrinkled like a prune. They may vary in color from a rich brick red to almost black. The dried peppers are ground into a powder or soaked for their pulp used in making red chile and other types of sauces.

The mulato chile is a different variety from the ancho, but when green looks just like it. The difference is that the mulato ripens to chocolate brown rather than red and may be larger.

Ancho chiles usually can only be purchased in the United States at stores devoted to Mexican foods. There you will find fresh green ones in season and the dried red ones the year around. Mulatos are more rarely found.

Just a few recipes in this book call for anchos because they are not widely available. These recipes specify "large dried mild red chiles (ancho, pasilla, or California)." You may use just one kind in these cases or mixtures of the three. In some stores, dried red California chiles may be called either ancho or pasilla. All three of these peppers have mild, sweet, and faintly hot flavors; that is why they may be used interchangeably.

Pasilla Chiles. (Pronounced "pah-*see*-yah") The true pasilla is a long, thin pepper from 7 to 12 inches long by about 1 or 1½ inches in diameter. It is dark green when immature, ripens to dark brown, becomes chocolate-brown when dried.

Read the preceding description of anchos for more detailed information about where to buy and how to use pasillas.

Poblano Chiles. (Pronounced "poh-*blah*-noh") Poblano is the term applied in certain areas of Mexico to the green form of the ancho or mulato.

In the United States where these peppers are not widely available, the California chile is substituted in poblano recipes. Bell peppers which resemble anchos can sometimes be used, but the fuller flavor of California chiles is better.

Chile Verde. (Pronounced "*vehr*-deh") This just means "green chile," referring to the immature or green form of various peppers.

However, sometimes grocers label particular kinds of chiles by this name, which results in much confusion. At various times or places, you might find fresh green California, Fresno, serrano, jalapeño, ancho, pasilla, mulato, or other peppers labelled chile verde. Occasionally, a merchant will insist that chile verde is the only true name of one particular variety.

Yellow Chiles. Several kinds may be sold either fresh or pickled. Among those you may encounter are the banana pepper, the Hungarian or the Armenian wax (both look something like a California chile), the Floral Gem, *caribe*, yellow wax (similar in size and shape to the green Fresno), and the *cascabel*.

MENUS FOR FIESTAS & FAMILY OCCASIONS

Tempting repasts geared to American tastes and customs

Mexican food is amazingly adaptable both to American entertaining and to everyday meals. Somehow it is festive, yet satisfying in a basic way. Several of the following menus will, therefore, be appreciated by sophisticated guests and children alike. These menus have still another appealing feature—most of the dishes can be made partly or completely ahead.

Summer Buffet
FOR 8 PEOPLE

Although the foods in this menu are from recipes collected in Mexico, they are more subtly seasoned than many traditional foods.

CHILE AND CHEESE SANDWICH

Recipe on page 53

MEXICAN WHITE RICE

Recipe on page 79

KIDNEY BEAN SALAD

Recipe on page 73

ORANGE SALAD

Recipe on page 74

CHEESE-CURRANT DESSERT TURNOVERS

Recipe on page 84

TROPICAL FRUIT PUNCH

Recipe on page 93

Preparation of the sandwich should begin the day before because the chiles should marinate for eight hours. Use the large, dried red chiles called *pasillas*, *anchos*, or California chiles. The chiles, and perhaps the dry jack cheese required, will necessitate a trip to a Mexican market.

Dinner for Guests
FOR 8 TO 12 PEOPLE

If you aren't sure whether or not your guests like Mexican foods, this menu provides a way to introduce authentic dishes with flavors that are familiar to or readily accepted by most people.

FISH APPETIZER, ACAPULCO STYLE

Recipe on page 66

CHICKEN WITH RICE

Recipe on page 61

HOT, SOFT CORN OR FLOUR TORTILLAS

Instructions on page 29, column 2

MANGO CREAM

Recipe on page 87

ORANGE SANGRÍA

Recipe on page 94

The fish appetizer, called Seviche, is a cocktail of raw fish "cooked" without benefit of heat. Don't be put off by the idea of raw fish—citrus juice thoroughly cooks it, strange as that may seem.

If you are serving 12 people, you should double the chicken recipe to have ample servings. The dish is garnished with peas and asparagus, so no additional vegetables are necessary.

Carne Asada Dinner
FOR 6 PEOPLE

This menu is based on one served by a Guadalajara restaurant famed for the variety and excellence of its Carnes Asadas.

CARNE ASADA BARBECUE

With sautéed green peppers and fried bananas
Recipe on page 58

RED OR GREEN SALSA JALAPEÑA

GREEN ONIONS   HOT CHILES   OLIVES

HARD DINNER ROLLS   BUTTER

RED WINE OR BEER

MANGOES

Fresh or canned in syrup

The grilled meat can be cooked right at the table, making a meal suited for relaxed entertaining.

Thin pieces of beef and pork tenderloin and precooked, chile-spiced chorizo sausages are broiled quickly over very hot coals in a clay Mexican *brasero*, a Japanese *hibachi*, or other small barbecue.

As the pace of this cook-and-serve meal is by nature leisurely, you'll need to keep the two hot accompaniments—butter-browned bananas and sautéed green peppers—warm on an electric tray or candle warmer. Piquant chiles, olives, onions, and hot sauce that you buy need only to be arranged and served.

It will add to the fun if your cooking utensil is a brasero, which typically resembles a primitive mask. Made of hard-fired black Oaxacan pottery or terra cotta, braseros are still used as stoves in some villages of Mexico, primarily in the south. Look for them in Mexican import shops.

Braseros don't come with grills, so use one from a small barbecue, have one made at a metal shop to fit the top bowl, or use a large round cake rack.

Guard against rapid changes in temperature. In the top bowl build a small fire, using no more than 10 briquets, to allow the temperature to rise slowly and prevent cracking (as a precautionary measure, it is wise to be outdoors the first time you use your brasero in case it does crack). Never transfer burning coals to a cold brasero. Store the brasero in a dry place.

Twelfth Night Party
FOR 12 PEOPLE

Twelfth Night or the Day of the Three Kings, January 6, is when Mexican children traditionally put out their shoes to receive Christmas gifts from the passing Magi. You may want to adapt some of the customs observed on this holiday for Christmas celebrations.

THREE KINGS' BREAD

Recipe on page 81

FRIED SWEET PUFFS (BUÑUELOS)

Recipe on page 90

ASSORTMENT OF FRESH FRUIT AND CHEESES

HOT CIDER

One of the most charming Twelfth Night customs has to do with the Three Kings' Bread, a fruit-studded yeast bread traditionally served on this day. A tiny doll or a large dry lima bean is baked into Three Kings' Bread, and whoever finds it in his piece is king or queen for the evening. However, he also has the responsibility of giving another party for everyone present; to avoid doing so, recipients of the "prize" have been known to swallow it. To assure a party in the future, use a doll or lima bean too large to be gulped down.

Buñuelos are also a traditional Christmas-time sweet.

A custom which could be incorporated into your party is the breaking of a *piñata*. These are gaily-decorated thin-walled clay pots, which are filled with candy and toys. The piñata is hung from a beam or tree branch so that blindfolded children can take turns swinging at it with a stick. When it finally breaks, the contents spill to the ground and the children rush to gather them up. Piñatas can be purchased in import stores.

Winter Buffet

FOR 10 TO 12 PEOPLE

One of the most festive of Mexican dishes, Turkey Mole with sauce of many spices, is the star of this buffet suitable for winter holiday occasions.

GUACAMOLE WITH POMEGRANATE SEEDS

Recipe on page 21

CORN TORTILLA CHIPS

Purchased or made by instructions on page 30

TURKEY MOLE

Recipe on page 61

STEAMED RICE

PUFFY FRIED BREAD

Recipe on page 82

GREEN SALAD

BAKED PINEAPPLE, NATILLAS

Recipe on page 85

LIME SANGRÍA FLOAT

Recipe on page 94

Crisp tortilla chips are used to scoop up the colorful Guacamole appetizer. The Puffy Fried Bread made of wheat flour, to accompany the turkey, offers a change from tortillas.

The dessert features baked fresh pineapple with a custard sauce.

The red-and-white Sangría wine drink is particularly suited to holiday entertaining. It may be served with the appetizer. You might want to serve a dry red wine throughout the meal.

Party Brunch

FOR 8 TO 12 PEOPLE

This hearty menu is easy to serve as a lap-tray meal. Hot tortillas are placed on warmed dinner plates and topped with generous servings of scrambled eggs; eat them with forks or roll and hold in the fingers. Thick slices of oven-baked bacon go alongside.

Mildly spiced black beans, baked for hours, can be eaten from bowls or cups, served over the eggs like a sauce, or rolled up in hot tortillas. Fresh to-

mato sauce, made hot as you like with chiles, is the topping for everything.

HOT, SOFT CORN TORTILLAS TOPPED WITH SCRAMBLED EGGS

Instructions for heating Tortillas on page 29

BAKED THICK-SLICED BACON

See instructions below

OAXACAN BAKED BLACK BEANS

Recipe on page 78

TOMATO AND GREEN CHILE SAUCE

Recipe on page 20

Use two or three eggs for each serving of eggs. Allow three or four tortillas per person. For eight servings, use two pounds smoked bacon, cut at least $1/4$-inch thick. Place it in a single layer on a rack in a pan and bake in a 275° oven along with the beans for $2^1/2$ to 3 hours, or until browned and crisp. Drain and serve hot.

Taco Picnic

FOR 6 TO 8 PEOPLE

This is a particularly colorful meal, simple to prepare. Hot, soft corn tortillas are wrapped around Carnitas, a succulent treatment of fresh pork called "little meats," to form Tacos. No plates or silverware are required except for serving, a real asset for a picnic meal.

TACOS WITH "LITTLE MEATS" PORK

Meat recipe on page 24
Tortilla heating and packing instructions on page 29

GUACAMOLE

Recipe on page 21

HOT REFRIED BEANS

Canned or made from recipe on page 22

SHREDDED LETTUCE, GREEN ONIONS, RADISHES, CARROT STICKS, PICKLED MILD CHILES

TROPICAL FRUITS WITH FRESH LIME

Prepared by following instructions

CHILLED ORANGE JUICE

To make the Tacos, hold a warm tortilla in the palm of your hand and fill it with a portion of meat and any of the vegetable relishes, Guaca-mole, or Refried Beans; fold the tortilla around this combination.

Dessert is also a hand-held operation. Cut pieces of fresh fruit—pineapple, papaya, coconut, banana—and squeeze a little lime juice over each portion.

You can cook the meat while organizing the rest of the meal at home. Since it can be served warm or at room temperature, no refrigeration is required. Heat the Refried Beans and transport them in a vacuum bottle. The Guacamole, raw vegetables, and orange juice should be kept cold.

Instructions for packing tortillas so they will stay hot enroute are also on page 29.

Midnight Christmas Eve Supper
FOR 6 TO 8 PEOPLE

This menu is a colorful choice for the adventure-some cook who wants to offer a festive meal that is Mexican throughout.

HOT CHEESE-TORTILLA APPETIZERS
Recipe on page 66

CHRISTMAS EVE SALAD
Recipe on page 72

TRIPE AND HOMINY SOUP
Recipe on page 69

HOT, SOFT CORN OR FLOUR TORTILLAS
Instructions on page 29, column 2

PUMPKIN-RAISIN DESSERT TURNOVERS
Recipe on page 84

HOT CHOCOLATE
Recipe on page 93

The appetizers may be served with your choice of drinks throughout an evening's celebration.

Other menu items comprise an amply filling midnight supper.

The salad is traditionally served on Christmas eve and the soup is a traditional late-night snack at any time.

The turnovers, with filling much like that of American holiday pies, can be made ahead and reheated if you like.

Steak Jalisco Barbecue
FOR 6 PEOPLE

This menu could serve for either a company or family dinner. The steak is a fairly large cut which could provide leftovers for another meal.

BEEFSTEAK JALISCO
Recipe on page 59

SOUR CREAM ENCHILADAS
Recipe on page 40

PICO DE GALLO SALAD
Either orange or jícama version
Recipes on page 73

FRESH PAPAYA OR CANTALOUPE
With lime wedges

The Enchilada casserole can be assembled early in the day and then put in the oven to bake at the same time you start cooking the meat.

The orange version of Pico de Gallo is made with ingredients readily obtainable. To make the other, you must be able to find the root vegetable called jícama.

Brunch or Almuerzo
FOR 4 (RECIPES EASILY DOUBLED)

Chilaquiles, hot and creamy with egg and cheese, can be served on thinly sliced lettuce. The crisp tortilla strips which go into the dish can be fried a day ahead if you want to simplify the final assembly. Leftover cooked turkey or chicken could be added, replacing the bacon on the menu.

CHILAQUILES
Recipe on page 34

CRISP BACON

FRESH PAPAYA OR CANTALOUPE
With lime wedges

HOT CHOCOLATE WITH CINNAMON STICKS
Recipe on page 93

Serve the fruit with the meal or as a separate course before or after. Sticks of cinnamon swirled into the hot chocolate are tasty and aromatic.

BASIC SAUCES & TYPICAL FILLINGS

Old standbys Mexican cooks use with scores of dishes

To prepare Mexican sauces, put aside any concepts of French-style sauce-making you may have acquired. You will not have to contend with the problems of simmered stocks, delicate seasonings, tendencies to curdle or lump, special cooking equipment, or gourmet guests who know the difference between a proper Hollandaise and a flop.

The sauces of Mexico were not devised by chefs with palates so pampered they can detect an extra sprig of tarragon in the Béarnaise or the vineyard from which their wine came. They were improvised by primitive people or peasants, with simple cooking facilities and no refrigeration, who needed to use what food they had on hand and often did not have too much on hand at that.

The sauces reflect their origin. They are earthy, hearty, richly seasoned, and filling. They keep well and are adaptable to many kinds of dishes. Accurate measurements and skilled techniques are not necessary to produce satisfactory results. There are as many variations as there are cooks who work by feel, handfuls, and pinches of this and that.

Add your own touches to the recipes which follow with confidence. The results will still probably be "authentic," for surely somewhere at some time a Mexican cook has already made the same kind of alteration.

Some of these sauces, particularly the thick, moist ones of meat or beans, are used more as fillings—in Tacos, Tamales, Enchiladas, or other typical, but lesser-known, specialties. All of the sauces and fillings in this chapter have a variety of uses, and most are specified in a number of recipes.

All of these, with one exception, can be made a day or more ahead of the time they are used. The exception is Guacamole, the mashed fresh avocado mixture which has become so popular in the United States as a cocktail dip.

Adjust the seasoning in all these sauces and fillings to your taste. Make them just as bland or peppery as you want. In Mexico as elsewhere, some like it hot and some don't.

Tomato & Green Chile Sauce

SALSA CRUDA (*sahl*-sah *kroo*-thah)

A bowl of sauce often is a standard feature on the Mexican table. Serve this colorful fresh sauce for each person to spoon onto his food to suit his own taste. You can make it as hot as you like, depending on the number of chiles you use.

6 medium-sized tomatoes
½ cup (or more) thinly sliced or diced canned
  California green chiles (seeds and pith
  removed) or fresh chiles (first peeled by
  method on page 14)
⅓ cup minced onion
1 teaspoon salt
  Minced canned *jalapeño* chiles (or other
  hot chiles) to taste

Peel and finely chop the tomatoes. Mix with California green chiles, onion, salt, and as many jalapeño chiles as please your taste (about 1 jalapeño to each cup of sauce will make it noticeably hot). Makes 3 cups.

Guacamole

(guah-kah-*moh*-leh)

Even the person who is indifferent to avocado in other forms is apt to become an avid Guacamole fan. Serve this mixture as a dip for crisp tortilla triangles, a salad, a tortilla filling, or a garnish. (Restaurants have used a cake decorator to pipe borders of it onto Enchilada platters or other baked dishes. If you do this, whirl the Guacamole in a blender first so it will go through the decorator smoothly.)

Season the basic avocado mixture to suit your own taste, but the citrus juice is a must—it keeps the avocado from discoloring.

Taco Picnic menu (page 18) and Winter Buffet menu (page 18) include this dish.

2 large ripe avocados
2 to 3 tablespoons lemon or lime juice,
    or to taste
Salt to taste, about ½ teaspoon
Optional: ½ teaspoon ground coriander seed
    or 2 teaspoons minced *cilantro* (sometimes
    called Chinese parsley or fresh coriander)
Optional: 2 to 4 canned California green
    chiles (rinsed, seeded, and chopped)
    and/or cayenne, liquid hot-pepper
    seasoning, or minced hot green chiles
    (*jalapeño, serrano,* and others) to taste

Cut avocados in half, remove seeds, and scoop out pulp with a spoon, or peel. Mash pulp coarsely with a fork while blending in lemon or lime juice. Add salt and coriander, if used. Add the chopped chiles, cayenne, or pepper seasoning if you'd like a touch of heat. Makes about 1²/₃ cups Guacamole.

Variations. Add 1 clove of garlic, minced or mashed, 2 or 3 tablespoons minced onion, or both garlic and onion.

Blend mayonnaise into the mixture to give it a smoother consistency.

Mix in 1 pimiento, chopped, or as much as 1 tomato, chopped.

For a festive appearance, garnish with tomato wedges and cilantro or parsley sprigs, or sprinkle pomegranate seeds over the top.

Red Chile Sauce

SALSA DE CHILE ROJO (theh *chee*-leh *rrroh*-hoh)

Dip tortillas in this cooked sauce to make Enchiladas, moisten meat fillings with it, or serve it as a condiment with meats. You can buy a similar sauce in cans, but the result of making your own is milder, thicker, and more flavorful—and you can freeze part to use later. Preparing the chiles is somewhat messy if you don't have a blender. Be sure to get the right dried chiles—large, dusky-red, mild ones—usually found only at stores specializing in Mexican foods.

6 ounces (about 10 to 12) whole dried *ancho,*
    pasilla, or California chiles (or a mixture
    of each)
3 cups hot water
¼ cup tomato sauce or tomato paste
1 small clove garlic, minced or mashed
¼ cup salad oil
1½ teaspoons salt
1 teaspoon crumbled oregano
¼ teaspoon ground cumin

Place chiles on a baking sheet. Toast lightly in a 400° oven for 3 or 4 minutes only, or until they give off a mild aroma. Do not burn the chiles or they will be very bitter.

Remove from oven, let cool to touch, then remove and discard stems, seeds, and any pink pithy material inside the chiles. Rinse in cool water, drain briefly, then cover chiles with hot water; let stand 1 hour.

Place chiles in a blender with enough of the water to blend; whirl until smooth. (Or scrape the pulp from the skin with a table knife, then put through a wire strainer.) Add remaining water, tomato sauce or tomato paste, garlic, salad oil, salt, oregano, and cumin. Simmer sauce gently for 10 minutes, stirring occasionally. You can freeze this sauce. Makes 3½ cups.

Chile-Tomato Sauce

Because you use chile powder instead of making a paste from dried chiles, this sauce is easy to prepare. The recipe makes enough sauce for 20 Enchiladas.

    1 medium-sized onion, minced
    2 tablespoons salad oil
 3½ cups tomato purée
    2 cloves garlic, minced or mashed
    4 tablespoons chile powder
  ½ teaspoon ground cumin seed
  ¼ teaspoon dried oregano
    1 teaspoon salt

Sauté onion in salad oil just until limp and yellow. Add tomato purée and garlic. Gradually stir in chile powder. Add cumin seed, oregano, and salt. Cover and simmer at least 30 minutes, stirring frequently. Strain through a medium-fine wire strainer. Makes about 3 cups.

Green Tomatillo Sauce
SALSA DE TOMATILLO (toh-mah-*tee*-yoh)

This subtly flavored, thick meat sauce is quite simple to make if you can find the necessary canned *tomatillos* (small, sweet green tomatoes).

Don't try to substitute ordinary green tomatoes—they do not have the proper sweet, mild taste.

For an entrée, heat cooked pork, turkey, or chicken in the sauce according to the recipe on page 60; or serve the sauce separately with roasts or grilled meats. It is complementary to beef, lamb, and particularly venison.

    1 medium-sized onion, finely chopped
  ¼ cup finely chopped blanched almonds
    2 tablespoons salad oil
    2 cans (10 oz. *each*) *tomatillos*
    1 tablespoon minced *cilantro* (also called
          Chinese parsley or fresh coriander) *or*
       1 teaspoon ground coriander seed
       About 3 tablespoons minced canned
          California green chiles (seeds and pith
          removed)—more or less, according to the
          chile flavor desired
    2 cups regular-strength chicken broth

Combine the onion, almonds, and oil in a saucepan and cook, stirring, over moderate heat until onion is soft and almonds are lightly browned.

Whirl the tomatillos and their liquid in a blender until mixture is fairly smooth (or rub through a wire strainer, using all liquid and pulp); add to onions. Stir in the coriander and chiles; taste to determine how much of the chile you want. The sauce should be fairly mild.

Add the chicken broth and simmer rapidly, uncovered, until reduced to 2½ cups; stir occasionally. You can cover sauce and chill as long as several days.

Refried Beans
FRIJOLES REFRITOS (free-*hoh*-less rrreh-*free*-tohs)

Undoubtedly it is because they are so economical that Refried Beans go into so many Mexican dishes. But that's certainly not the only reason—they are also delicious and keep well refrigerated. Serve them as a starchy accompaniment or as a filling for Tacos, Enchiladas, Tostadas, Flautas, and the other dishes in this book which call for Refried Beans.

You can use the canned variety, heated with a little butter, bacon drippings, or lard if you like more richness. The canned beans improve in flavor and texture if they are stirred in a pan over low heat a few minutes, or even "refried" with the additional fat. Or you can make your own from the following recipe.

Taco Picnic menu includes Refried Beans (see page 18).

    1 pound dried pinto or pink beans, cleaned
    5 cups water
    1 or 2 medium-sized onions, diced (optional)
  ½ to 1 cup hot bacon drippings, butter, or lard
       Salt to taste

Combine beans in a pan with water and onions. Bring to a boil, cover, and remove from heat for 2 hours (or soak beans in cold water overnight). Return to heat, bring to a boil, and simmer slowly until beans are very tender, about 3 hours. Mash beans with a potato masher, and add bacon drippings, butter, or lard. Mix well; continue cooking, stirring frequently until beans are thickened and fat is absorbed. Salt to taste. Serve or reheat. Makes 6 to 8 side-dish servings, or 5 to 6 cups.

Homemade Link Chorizo Sausage

CHORIZO HECHO EN CASA
(choh-*ree*-soh *eh*-choh ehn *ka*-sah)

If you'd like your Mexican culinary specialties to be a bit out of the ordinary or if you live where chorizo sausages cannot be purchased, making your own may appeal to you. The sausages can be mild or more pungent, depending on how much chile powder you use. The salted pig casings necessary often are available in markets patronized by foreign-born shoppers. Or your meatman can order them for you.

```
   Sausage casings (enough for 20 four-inch
      sausages)
   Vinegar (optional)
 2 pounds pork
10 ounces pork or beef fat
 1 large onion, finely chopped
 6 cloves garlic, minced or mashed
 1 can (4 oz.) pimientos
 2 ounces (¼ cup) chile powder (or more)
½ cup vinegar
¼ cup brandy or tequila
 1 teaspoon freshly ground black pepper
 1 teaspoon cinnamon
1½ teaspoons ground cumin
2½ teaspoons salt
```

Soak the casings in warm water for 3 or 4 hours, then rinse them in running water (put one end over the end of the faucet and let the water run through). It is also a good idea to pour a cup of vinegar through the casings, so the sausage will keep better.

Grind pork through the coarse blade of food chopper. Finely dice fat (do not grind). Add other ingredients. For a hotter chorizo, add more chile powder; two ounces makes a mild chorizo, suitable to most American palates.

Mix all ingredients thoroughly. Cut prepared casing in 4-foot lengths for easier handling. Tie one end of each length; press out all air through the other end; and fill with chorizo mixture, using a funnel, cake decorator without tube attached, or sausage-stuffing machine. (*See photo in next column.*) Tie every 4 inches.

Hang sausages to dry for 24 hours in a breezy spot outdoors or in the house with an electric fan blowing on them. They will keep, refrigerated, for several weeks. Makes 20 sausages.

CHORIZO LINKS are made by forcing meat into a pork casing with a cake decorator, then tying with string.

Simple Chorizo Sausage Filling

RELLENO DE CHORIZO (rrreh-*yeh*-noh)

The spicy link sausage called *chorizo* is made of pork and beef heavily spiced with garlic, chile powder, and other seasonings. The sausages vary considerably in chile pepper "hotness," in fat content, and even in size. You'll find them in many supermarkets or in Mexican and specialty food stores.

To make the Simple Chorizo Filling called for in several recipes in this book, peel off and discard the casing. Crumble or chop the meat and then brown the meat in a frying pan. Pour off any excess fat.

If you'd like a less spicy filling, you can combine chorizo with as much browned ground beef as needed to give the flavor you want. Add some Mexican red chile sauce to moisten, if you wish.

If you cannot find chorizos to buy, you can either make link chorizos at home by the preceding recipe or prepare the Bulk Chorizo Sausage Filling (recipe on next page), which is made with ground meats and spices.

Bulk Chorizo Sausage Filling

RELLENO SUELTO DE CHORIZO (suel-toh)

The heavily spiced sausage that is such a popular filling for tortilla dishes doesn't come just in link form. In parts of Mexico and the Southwest you can also buy chorizo as a fresh ground mixture in bulk form. You can make your own similar chorizo mixture from this recipe.

    1 large onion, finely chopped
    1 pound ground beef
    ½ pound ground pork butt
    2 teaspoons *each* chile powder and
         crumbled oregano
    ½ teaspoon ground cumin
    ¼ teaspoon cinnamon
    1 teaspoon salt
    ½ teaspoon liquid hot-pepper seasoning
         (optional)
    5 tablespoons vinegar
   1½ cups canned Enchilada sauce

Combine the onion, ground beef, ground pork, chile powder, oregano, cumin, cinnamon, salt, hot-pepper seasoning, and vinegar. To prepare this mixture as a filling, lightly brown it in a wide frying pan over medium-high heat, breaking the meat apart as it cooks. Add Enchilada sauce and boil rapidly until liquid is gone.

Ground Beef Filling

RELLENO DE CARNE PICADA
(rrreh-*yeh*-noh theh *kar*-neh pee-*kah*-thah)

Browned ground beef, seasoned with onion and red chile sauce, makes a tasty all-purpose filling for Tacos, Enchiladas, and Tostadas.

    1 pound lean ground beef
    1 or 2 tablespoons salad oil or lard (optional)
    1 medium-sized onion, chopped
    ½ cup Red Chile Sauce (recipe on page 21),
         or canned Mexican red chile or Enchilada
         sauce

In a frying pan, break apart and brown the ground beef, adding salad oil or lard if needed. Add onion and cook until soft. Moisten with red chile or Enchilada sauce. Slowly simmer for 10 minutes, stirring occasionally. Makes 3 cups.

Pork or Chicken Filling

RELLENO DE CARNE DE PUERCO (puer-koh)
RELLENO DE POLLO (poh-yoh)

The mild flavor of cooked pork or poultry combines well with both the sweetness of raisins and the spiciness of chiles.

   1½ tablespoons salad oil or melted lard
    1 medium-sized onion, chopped
    2 cups finely diced or shredded cooked
         lean pork, cooked chicken, or cooked
         turkey
    1 small canned *jalapeño* chile or other
         pickled very hot chile, minced (optional)
    ¼ cup raisins
   1½ tablespoons chopped ripe olives
    ⅔ cup Red Chile Sauce (recipe on Page 21),
         or canned Mexican red chile or
         Enchilada sauce

In hot salad oil or lard, sauté onion until limp. Blend in pork, chicken, or turkey; chile; raisins; olives; and sauce. Simmer 10 minutes, stirring occasionally. Makes 2½ to 3 cups.

"Little Meats" Pork

CARNITAS (kar-*nee*-tas)

The name of this succulent dish means "little meats." The pork is so tender it is easily cut into chunks or shredded into little pieces good for a Taco filling. It also can be served like a roast.

Taco Picnic menu includes this (see page 18).

   4½ to 5-pound pork shoulder (do not have the
         bone cut)
       Water
    2 teaspoons salt
    ½ teaspoon *each* crumbled oregano, ground
         cumin, and ground or crushed whole
         coriander
    2 medium-sized onions, chopped
    2 carrots, chopped

Place the pork shoulder in a deep pan and just barely cover with water. Add the salt, oregano, cumin, coriander, onions, and carrots. Bring water to a boil, cover pan, and simmer meat gently for 2½ hours. Lift meat from stock (save for soups) and place in a baking pan.

Bake in a 350° oven for 45 minutes to 1 hour or until meat is very well browned. Drain off all fat.

TORTILLA-MAKING & TORTILLA DISHES

How to serve as bread or use in preparing popular treats

When the ancient Mexicans invented *tortillas*—their flat, round, unleavened bread—they invented the most versatile bread of all. A bread that can be stacked, rolled, folded, torn, cut, and crumbled. A bread that tastes good soft and hot, crisply fried, or toasted. A bread that can be shaped with the hands and easily baked on an improvised griddle over any source of heat, that keeps well, and that can be reheated later.

What they invented even substitutes for eating utensils when used as a scoop or replaces a plate when laid in the palm of the hand and filled with food.

The tortilla is a food born out of the necessities of primitive people. The first ones were made of the native corn, dried to keep until the next crop came in. The kernels were simmered in water with lime until partially soft (this is called *nixtamal*), then laboriously ground by hand on a stone mortar called a *metate*. The moist meal, called *masa*, was patted into a thin pancake and baked on a *comal* (a clay griddle).

When the Spaniards introduced wheat flour, cooks quickly turned that into tortillas, too, although they did not become as widely used and now are more a specialty of the northern part of the country.

Today the ways of preparing tortillas have changed somewhat in the more urban areas. Machines may grind the corn and wheat, and occasionally machines may shape, bake, and even freeze the product. The moist masa sometimes is dehydrated and sold in bags like flour, to later be mixed with water at home.

In the United States, neoned Taco stands and supermarkets peddle the tortilla and chic hostesses may serve tortilla chips, bought in paper bags, to scoop up cocktail dips.

But the corn tortilla made most places in modern Mexico is little different from that the Mexican Indians made hundreds of years ago. A few sophisticated cooks may add refinements which work small improvements in certain dishes. However, in the market places, bread is still made the old way. There you will see women working huge white mounds of masa, which oozes excess liquid, until the dough has just the right feel. Then they slap and pat it into cakes and bake them on the spot.

The slap-slap sounds of many tortilla-makers at work and the heady scent of cooking corn are sensual experiences of the real Mexico which many visitors long remember.

Tortillas are so basic to Mexican cookery that an understanding of how to buy or make them and the various ways of cooking them will help anyone preparing recipes from this book to have greater success.

All the recipes in this book specify whether corn or flour tortillas should be used.

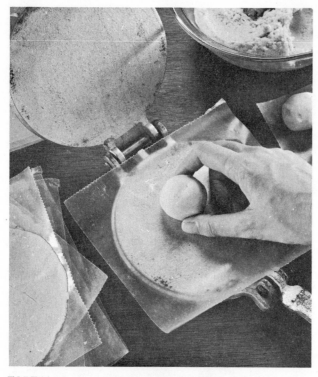

TORTILLAS are quickly formed from dough with a modern metal press and waxed paper to prevent sticking.

PRESS slowly and firmly to flatten dough. Leave tortilla on waxed paper until ready to bake on griddle.

HOW TO BUY TORTILLAS

In most food stores in the West, both corn and flour tortillas are sold, usually by the dozen in a plastic-wrapped package (or sometimes in a box or can). They will usually be found either in a refrigerated area of the store, in a freezer, or on the shelf if canned.

Corn tortillas are usually six inches in diameter, flour ones 7 inches or much larger.

Frozen tortillas keep almost indefinitely under ideal freezing temperature (0 degrees or colder), but do lose their flavor and moisture within a matter of weeks or several months in refrigerator freezing compartments at higher temperatures. Those which are not frozen may be kept refrigerated for several days, or frozen at home for somewhat longer storage.

Thaw frozen tortillas before reheating by separating them, brushing off ice crystals, and laying them flat. They will thaw in about 5 minutes; if you do not use right away, cover with foil or plastic wrap to keep them from drying out.

The quality of tortillas you buy can vary considerably. If you want the best cooking results, compare the brands available to you. If you buy unfrozen tortillas, be sure they are fresh. Bend the package to see that the bread is still tender and flexible; it should not look dry around the edges.

The tortillas you buy have already been cooked. But to serve them as bread or to use them in cooking, you will need to reheat or fry them. Pages 29 and 30 are devoted to the various ways this may be done.

HOW TO MAKE TORTILLAS

If you live in an area where ready-made tortillas are not sold or if you want the pleasure and superior results of making your own, recipes follow in this chapter for making both the corn and flour types.

Flour tortillas can be made from the regular all-purpose flour you have on hand. But corn tortillas require the special corn preparation called Masa Harina (dehydrated masa flour), if you do not have access to fresh masa. Do not try to make tortillas with regular corn meal, which is too coarsely ground and prepared differently than the corn for masa.

Masa Harina is sold in five-pound (or larger) bags at stores specializing in Mexican or gourmet foods. As it also is used for Tamales and other specialties and keeps like flour, it would be wise to buy an ample supply when you locate a source. For information about where Masa Harina is sold, see page 10.

Both flour and corn tortillas can be patted into shape by hand, but the technique is something best learned at a Mexican mother's knee. Lacking such upbringing, you may roll the dough with a rolling pin, trimming each tortilla to an even round if you wish. For quickest and best results, you may want to invest in an inexpensive tortilla press (prices range from $3 to $6) or even make one according to the instructions following.

HOMEMADE TORTILLA PRESS

A tortilla press which works well can be easily made from a few scraps of lumber. And the rougher your woodworking, the more authentic it looks. *See diagram below.*

Use any ³⁄₄ to 1-inch-thick wood on hand, choosing unwarped boards that will fit together evenly. Cut the paddle-shaped bottom from an 8¹⁄₂ by 12¹⁄₂-inch piece, leaving a handle on one end where you attach the 2 by 2 pressure arm. Glue and nail four 1 by 2 crosspieces to the top and bottom boards to help prevent warping when the press is washed. Attach hinges securely with long screws.

Last, locate the arm's ¹⁄₄-inch bolt at a height where the arm can lever down (not completely horizontal) over the top of the press.

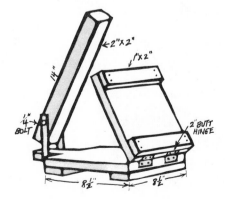

Corn Tortillas

TORTILLAS DE MAIZ (tor-*tee*-yahs deh mah-*ees*)

See preceding section, How to Make Tortillas, for information about Masa Harina. Photos on the opposite page show use of a Tortilla press.

> 2 cups Masa Harina (dehydrated masa flour)
> 1¹⁄₃ cups warm water

Mix masa flour with warm water until dough holds together well. Using your hands, shape dough into a smooth ball. Divide dough into 12 equal-sized pieces, then roll each into a ball.

Tortilla Press Method of Shaping. Place a square of waxed paper on bottom half of tortilla press; place 1 ball of dough on the paper, slightly off center toward the edge farthest from the handle. Flatten it slightly with the palm of your hand. Cover with a second square of waxed paper. Lower top half of the press (being careful not to wrinkle the paper), and press down firmly on lever until the tortilla measures about 6 inches in diameter. Stack paper-covered dough and cook according to following instructions.

Rolling Pin Method of Shaping. Use two cloths which have been dipped in water and wrung dry. Flatten a ball of dough slightly and place between the cloths. Roll with light, even strokes until the cake is about 6 inches in diameter. Carefully pull back cloths, trim tortilla to a round shape if necessary, and sandwich it between two squares of waxed paper. Roll out all the dough balls similarly. Cook according to instructions.

Cooking Instructions. Peel off top piece of waxed paper carefully. Invert the tortilla, paper side up, onto a preheated, ungreased, medium-hot griddle or into a heavy frying pan over medium-high heat. As the tortilla becomes warm, you will be able to peel off the remaining paper.

Bake, turning frequently, until the tortilla looks dry and is lightly flecked with brown specks (it should still be soft), 1¹⁄₂ to 2 minutes.

Serve tortillas immediately while still warm, or cool and wrap airtight. Store airtight packages in refrigerator or freezer. To serve, reheat or fry by method described on pages 29 and 30. Makes 1 dozen 6-inch tortillas.

Flour Tortillas

TORTILLAS DE HARINA (ah-*ree*-nah)

The flour tortillas you buy are 7 inches in diameter, or much larger, and about the same thickness as corn ones (1/16 of an inch or so). For most purposes in this book, you will want to make the 7-inch size.

However, in Sonora where they use flour more than corn, the flour version often is made as large as 18 inches in diameter and paper thin. Cooks stretch and pat the dough to these proportions, or flip it the way Italians make pizza; but you will probably prefer to use a rolling pin.

The large tortillas are great fun at barbecues or picnics cooked the way some Sonorans do them, on the top of an oil drum with a hot wood fire inside. Instructions follow the recipe for making your own oil-drum griddle, undoubtedly a necessity if you want to make Tortillas de Harina a foot-and-a-half wide.

This recipe will make about 11 regular-sized or 8 giant-sized, thin ones. A properly cooked flour tortilla remains mostly white, but is flecked with brown and puffed in spots; it has a dry look but still is soft and pliable.

    2 cups unsifted flour
    1 teaspoon salt
    ¼ cup lard
    ½ cup lukewarm water
       Lard

Put flour in mixing bowl, sprinkle with salt, stir to mix. With pastry blender or two knives, cut in lard until particles are fine. Add water gradually; toss with a fork to make a stiff dough. Form into a ball and knead thoroughly until smooth and flecked with air bubbles on a lightly floured board.

At this point you can grease the surface of the dough, cover tightly, and refrigerate for as long as 24 hours before using; if you do this, the dough will be easier to handle. Let dough return to room temperature before you begin to roll it out.

Divide dough into 8 balls for large, thin tortillas or 11 balls for regular-sized, 7-inch tortillas. For large, thin tortillas, roll as thin as possible on a lightly floured board. (Or stretch and pat with floured hands until thin.) For regular-sized ones, roll between sheets of waxed paper to 8 inches diameter, adding flour as needed, and trim any ragged edges. Tortillas will shrink to 7 inches when cooked.

Drop onto a very hot ungreased griddle. Bake until freckled on one side. (This should take only about 20 seconds.) Lift edge with spatula, turn, and bake on second side.

To serve at once, fold hot, limp tortilla around pieces of butter.

Or cool tortillas, wrap airtight, and refrigerate or freeze. To serve later, reheat or fry by methods described on pages 29 and 30. Makes 11 seven-inch tortillas (1/16 inch thick) or 8 giant-sized, paper-thin ones.

MAKING AN OIL-DRUM GRIDDLE

Ask your service station proprietor for a 15-gallon oil drum (there may be a small charge).

If the drum has a removable lid, you can build the fire in the bottom of the drum and use the lid as the griddle surface. If it hasn't a lid, or the lid is not removable, invert the drum and use the drum bottom as the griddle.

Drill exhaust holes and cut a door with a hack saw as shown in the diagram. The door may be hinged with wire and closed with the simple latch sketched below.

To clean drum, build a fire inside; this will burn out the oil and cause paint to peel off outside. When cool, scrub with steel wool, soap, and water. To season the griddle, brush the clean metal surface with salad oil and heat until the oil smokes. Wipe dry with paper towels.

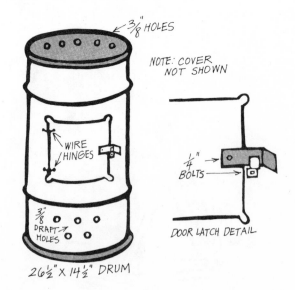

3/8" HOLES

NOTE: COVER NOT SHOWN

WIRE HINGES

3/8" DRAFT HOLES

26½" X 14½" DRUM

¼" BOLTS

DOOR LATCH DETAIL

Egg-Masa Tortillas

Ordinary tortillas made of corn masa and water will serve for all dishes you might prepare. But a California man has invented a tortilla that is a cross between the corn kind and a French pancake. It retains the full, husky tortilla flavor but has a moist tenderness ideal for Enchiladas.

 2 eggs
¾ cup milk
 1 tablespoon melted shortening
½ cup Masa Harina (dehydrated masa flour)
 2 tablespoons regular all-purpose wheat flour
¼ teaspoon salt

Beat together the eggs, milk, shortening, masa flour, wheat flour, and salt to make a smooth batter. Use 2 tablespoons batter for each tortilla. Dip a spoonful of batter onto a greased griddle, swirling the batter to round out the cake to a 5 or 6-inch diameter. Bake lightly on each side. Makes 10 tortillas.

HEATING & FRYING TORTILLAS

With any meal, you may serve whole, plain tortillas (corn or flour) as a bread. These are usually served soft and hot, preferably wrapped in a napkin to keep them moist and warm as long as possible. Both tortillas you make from scratch and those you buy can be prepared this way quickly if you follow directions carefully.

Instructions follow for preparing soft, hot tortillas on an ungreased surface or in hot oil. Sometimes they are buttered before serving and folded or rolled to keep the melted butter inside; extra butter may be served at the table. Or you may just provide butter for those who want it.

Corn tortillas provide a cracker-type accompaniment when crisp-fried in oil (instructions follow). They can be fried whole but are most convenient to serve if they are cut into wedges before cooking. These wedges can serve as dippers for Guacamole and other appetizers and as an accompaniment for soups or salads. They are best hot but are also palatable cold and will keep their crispness for several hours unwrapped.

Crisp-fried tortillas are called Tostadas, which means "toasted." Tostada also is the name of an entirely different thing—the popular dish with base of crisp tortilla piled high with meat, beans, shredded lettuce, cheese, and other things. To avoid confusion, whenever just the plain fried tortilla type of Tostada (cut in wedges) is meant, the recipes in this book also will refer to them as corn tortilla chips. (The Mexicans sometimes call them by the diminutive, Tostaditas, which would be the least confusing term if consistently used.)

You can also purchase the chips in bags at the potato-chip sections of many food markets, but for most occasions you will probably prefer to make them fresh.

The following sections will give you brief summaries of the varied techniques for preparing tortillas to serve as bread or crackers.

To Reheat and Soften Corn or Flour Tortillas on an Ungreased Surface. Fresh tortillas are already soft in a sense, but when heated they become even more tender and flexible. If tortillas are dry and a little hard, dip your hand in water and rub it lightly onto surfaces of the bread before heating. Be sure not to heat them longer than necessary to soften and warm thoroughly, or they will become hard and brittle.

Place tortillas so they do not overlap on a medium-hot griddle or in a heavy frying pan over medium-high heat. Turn *frequently* until soft and hot, about 30 seconds.

Put immediately into a tightly covered dish, or put into a foil packet and seal it, and hold in a 200° oven until all tortillas are heated. (The secret is to keep them from drying out once heated.)

How to Keep Soft Tortillas Hot Several Hours. Wrap hot tortillas airtight in foil and place in an insulated bag, or wrap the foil package in a cloth and then 12 or 14 sheets of newspaper. The tortillas will stay hot for at least 2 hours in the paper wrapping, and longer than that in the insulated bag. You can use this method for picnics or any occasion when it would be handy to prepare tortillas ahead of time.

To Soften Corn or Flour Tortillas by Frying. Heat about ¼ inch of salad oil, shortening, or lard in a frying pan over medium-high heat. Quickly turn one or two tortillas at a time in oil; they soften almost immediately. Do not allow them to become crisp. Drain on paper towels.

(Continued on next page)

To Toast Corn or Flour Tortillas. Place tortillas on a grill or in a hinged broiler 3 or 4 inches above a low flame or coals; cook, turning frequently with a fork or tongs, until tortillas are heated through, soft, and lightly blistered—this takes about a minute. Serve immediately.

To Heat Corn or Flour Tortillas in an Electronic Range. Stack tortillas on a paper towel; do not use foil. Six tortillas require 45 seconds to heat. A dozen tortillas (in two stacks of 6 each) heat in 1 minute.

To Crisp-Fry Whole Corn or Flour Tortillas. Heat 1 inch of salad oil, shortening, or lard in a frying pan to 350° to 375°. Fry one tortilla at a time, using a spatula to turn frequently or to hold it under the fat until it crisps, puffs slightly, and browns lightly (about 1 minute or less). Drain on paper towels.

To Crisp-Fry Corn Tortilla Chips (Called Tostadas or Tostaditas). Cut tortillas into pie-shaped wedges (4ths, 6ths, or 8ths). Heat about 1 inch of salad oil, shortening, or lard in a frying pan to 350° to 375°. Fry just a few at a time, turning occasionally, until crisp and lightly browned, about 1 minute or less. Drain on paper towels; sprinkle lightly with salt if desired. Store airtight.

Tacos
(*tah*-kos)

Although Tacos in the United States often are made of corn tortillas crisp-fried into a half-moon-shaped pocket, those in Mexico have much more variety. *See photo on opposite page.*

There they may be of either corn or flour tortillas, which often are just heated on a griddle until soft. Sometimes the tortillas are folded in half to hold the filling, but more often they are rolled all the way around it—a much neater arrangement for eating.

The word *taco* merely means a "snack," but in popular usage it has come to mean the tortilla-sandwich type of snack with meat filling, garnish, and spicy sauce.

Some other snack specialties are really just variations of a Taco. A Chimichanga is a flour tor-

tilla, usually a large one, wrapped around any variety of fillings and deep-fried until flaky. Quesadillas contain a cheese filling to which seasonings such as green chiles may be added; the tortilla may be open flat with the cheese melted on top, or folded over the cheese. (Quesadillas are also made with raw masa.) Flautas are made of two overlapping corn tortillas filled, rolled, and fried crisp. Recipes for these specific specialties are printed after this recipe for Tacos.

The following instructions will tell you how to make Tacos of great variety with a choice of meat fillings and garnishes. First comes information about the techniques for preparing both corn and flour tortillas, including how to heat them until soft and crisp-fry them for either folded or rolled Tacos. Then filling, garnish, and sauce suggestions are given.

It would take a mathematician to compute the number of Taco variations you will be able to prepare with these specific suggestions, not to mention those possible if you add your own ideas and innovations.

To Make Folded or Rolled Tacos with Soft Tortillas (Either Corn or Flour). For these Tacos, you want the tortillas to be piping hot, but still moist and flexible. The easiest way to soften them is to place them individually (not overlapping) on an ungreased medium-hot griddle or in a heavy frying pan over medium-high heat. Turn frequently until soft and hot, about 30 seconds. Wrap in cloth or foil immediately and keep in a warm place until ready to use.

You can prepare soft tortillas several hours ahead if packaged according to the instructions on page 29. At barbecues, you can toast them over coals (see top of left column).

Electronic ranges not only heat quickly but also leave the tortillas very moist and steamy (see left-hand column for instructions).

To make folded soft Tacos, just spoon fillings down the center of a hot tortilla, add garnishes and/or sauce, and fold one half of the bread over to make a semi-circular sandwich.

For rolled Tacos, roll one side of the tortilla over the fillings and keep rolling until you have a tubular shape.

To Make Folded, Crisp-Fried Tacos. This shape, made with corn tortillas, is the familiar form sold at Taco stands in the United States.

(Continued on next page)

TACOS can be made in two basic shapes (folded or rolled) and two forms (with soft or crisp-fried tortilla).

QUESADILLAS, tortillas fried crisp with cheese and chile filling, are one of the easiest specialties to make.

FLAUTAS are made like rolled Tacos, except that two overlapping tortillas are used, forming a long tube.

TOSTADAS can be two different foods—crisp tortilla chips (top) and open-faced tortilla sandwiches (below).

Fry one corn or flour tortilla at a time in about ¹/₂ inch of hot salad oil, lard, or shortening over medium heat, until it becomes soft (just a few seconds). Then fold it in half and hold slightly open with tongs or two forks so that there is a space between the halves for filling to be added later. Fry the tortilla until crisp and light brown, turning as necessary to cook all sides. The process only takes a total of several minutes.

To keep the half-moon-shaped Taco shells warm until ready to fill, you may put them on a paper-towel-lined baking sheet in a 200° oven for as long as 10 or 15 minutes.

To Make Rolled, Crisp-Fried Tacos. You must first soften a corn or flour tortilla by dipping it in hot oil for just a few seconds. Remove, drain on paper towels, and spoon the filling slightly off center, down one side of the tortilla. Fold one side over the filling and roll up.

To hold the filling in while you fry the Taco, secure the flap of the tortilla with a small skewer or a wooden toothpick, or hold it shut with tongs. Fry the roll over medium heat in at least ¹/₂ inch hot salad oil, shortening, or lard until light brown and crisp. Drain on paper towels, tilting so that excess oil can drain out of the center.

Some cooks believe it is easier to roll the tortillas without the filling, fry, and then fill with a small spoon. This keeps the filling from falling out during the cooking and from absorbing oil.

Taco Fillings. A variety of meat fillings used in many Mexican dishes make excellent Tacos. Because these mixtures are so basic and interchangeable, the recipes for them are in the Basic Sauces and Fillings Chapter. They are: Ground Beef, page 24; Simple Chorizo, page 23; Bulk Chorizo, page 24; Pork or Chicken, page 24; and "Little Meats" Pork (also called Carnitas), page 24.

You can also use any cooked meat (ground or shredded) seasoned with Taco sauce, Taco seasoning mix sold in 1¹/₄-ounce foil packets similar to those for salad dressing mixes, or onions sautéed in butter or oil. You can even use slivers or thin slices of leftover cold roast meats or fowl.

Sauces and Garnishes. Sauces may be mixed with the meat filling to moisten it if desirable, spooned on top of it, or poured on after garnishes are added. You can buy bottled Taco sauces, canned green chile salsa, and canned Mexican red chile sauce. Several homemade sauces are appropriate: Fresh Tomato and Green Chile Sauce, page 20; Red Chile Sauce, page 21; Chile-Tomato Sauce, page 22; and Green Tomatillo Sauce, page 22. You may also use Guacamole (page 21) or Refried Beans (canned or page 22) as sauces, but an additional spicy sauce on top of that is good for tang.

Shredded lettuce and shredded Cheddar or jack cheese are the two most popular garnishes. Other possibilities are chopped bulb or green onions, chopped tomatoes (or thin wedges), chopped mild chiles (canned or pickled), sliced or diced avocado, or chopped cilantro (also called fresh coriander or Chinese parsley).

Quesadillas
(keh-sah-*thee*-yas)

You come across a variety of foods called Quesadillas in Mexico. They all have cheese fillings, but the fillings are flavored in different ways. This is one of the easiest ways to prepare Quesadillas. *See photo on preceding page.*

 1 **can (7 oz.) California green chiles,**
   seeds and pith removed
 1 **pound jack cheese**
12 **corn or flour tortillas**
   Butter, lard, or salad oil for frying (optional)

To make each one, place about half a chile and a thick stick (about 1 by 4 by ¹/₂ inches) of jack cheese in the center of a tortilla. Fold tortilla over cheese and pin shut with a small wooden skewer.

Fry in shallow hot butter, lard, or salad oil until crisp, turning occasionally. Drain on paper towels. (Or just heat and soften the tortilla on each side on a medium-hot ungreased griddle or frying pan, until the cheese has melted.) Makes 12 Quesadillas.

Variation. To fill the tortillas, you may also shred the cheese (it melts more easily this way) and mix it with the chiles, cut in small pieces.

Chimichangas

(chee-mee-*chan*-gas)

A specialty of the state of Sonora, these are enormous Tacos made with the platter-sized flour tortillas common there. You can make a smaller version with regular-sized (7-inch) flour tortillas, which become flaky when fried.

     12 flour tortillas (7 inches in diameter)
     2¼ cups meat filling (Ground Beef, page 24)
          Salad oil, shortening, or lard for frying
     1½ to 2 cups *each* shredded Cheddar cheese,
          shredded lettuce, and chopped radishes
          or green onions

Spoon 3 tablespoons filling down the center of tortilla. Fold tortilla around filling, and fasten with wooden toothpicks. Assemble only 2 or 3 at a time, as the tortilla will absorb liquid from the sauce.

Fry in 1 inch of hot oil over medium heat (about 350°), turning, until golden; takes 1 to 2 minutes. Lift from fat with a slotted spoon, draining, then place on a thick layer of paper towels; keep in a warm place until all are cooked.

Serve garnished with 2 or 3 tablespoons *each* shredded cheese, lettuce, and radishes or green onions. Allow 2 or 3 for a main-dish serving. Makes 12 Chimichangas.

Flautas

(*flou*-tas)

The word *flauta*, meaning "flute," describes the tubular shape of this Taco variation. *See photo on page 31.*

     12 corn tortillas
          About 1½ cups meat filling (Ground Beef,
          page 24; Simple Chorizo, page 23;
          or Pork or Chicken, page 24)
          Salad oil, shortening, or lard for frying

For each Flauta, soften and heat 2 tortillas by turning them about 30 seconds each on an ungreased griddle over medium-high heat. Lay the tortillas flat and overlapping.

Spoon a band of 3 to 4 tablespoons warm meat filling across the greatest length of the overlapping cakes, then roll tortillas around filling. Hold shut with tongs (or fasten with small wooden

skewers), and fry over medium heat in about ½ inch of oil heated to 350° until the Flauta is slightly crisp. Drain on paper towels, then eat with your fingers.

(If you prefer, roll and fry the tortillas, then use a spoon to add the filling.) Makes 6 Flautas.

Tostadas

(tohs-*tah*-thas)

A whole crisp-fried tortilla makes the bottom layer of what is really an open-faced sandwich. The ingredients traditionally offer contrasts of soft and crisp, hot and cold, savory or sharp and mild. *See photo on page 31.*

     4 whole corn tortillas, crisp-fried by
          directions on page 30
     ¾ to 1 cup hot Refried Beans (canned or made
          by recipe on page 22)
     ½ cup shredded jack cheese
     ½ to ¾ cup shredded or thinly sliced cooked
          chicken, turkey, or pork, *or* Ground Beef
          Filling (recipe on page 24)
     1 to 2 cups shredded lettuce
          Chicken or pork slices for garnish (optional)
          Avocado slices or Guacamole (recipe on
          page 21)
          Red Chile Sauce (recipe on page 21)   or
          Fresh Tomato and Green Chile Sauce
          (recipe on page 20)

For each Tostada, spread a fried tortilla with about 3 to 4 tablespoons hot Refried Beans, sprinkle with about 2 tablespoons cheese, cover with about 2 or 3 tablespoons meat, top with about ¼ to ½ cup shredded lettuce, and garnish with a few pieces of meat and avocado slices or about 3 tablespoons Guacamole. Serve with sauce. Makes 4 Tostadas (4 servings).

Crab Tostadas
TOSTADAS DE CANGREJO (kahn-*greh*-hoh)

One Mexican restaurant in San Francisco makes a specialty of this hot seafood Tostada. It is served in a low, round basket.

    1 avocado, peeled and seeded
    2 tablespoons lime juice
    ¼ teaspoon garlic salt
    1 large head iceberg lettuce
    1 can (1 lb. 4 oz.) Refried Beans
    4 whole corn tortillas, crisp-fried by
        directions on page 30
    1 cup shredded mild Cheddar cheese
    ¾ to 1 pound crab meat
    2 medium-sized tomatoes, sliced
    ½ cup pitted ripe olives
        Canned or bottled Taco sauce

Mash avocado and blend in the lime juice and garlic salt.

Line four plates with the outer lettuce leaves, then finely shred the inside head and mound on the plates. Heat the beans until they start to bubble. Arrange a crisp tortilla on top of the greens on each plate, and spoon over the hot beans. Sprinkle with cheese, and cover with a layer of crab meat (save some for garnish).

Spoon on avocado mixture; garnish with crab pieces. Surround with sliced tomatoes and ripe olives. Pass a pitcher of sauce. Makes 4 Tostadas (4 servings).

Chilaquiles
(chee-lah-*kee*-less)

The casserole dishes of varying ingredients called Chilaquiles are leftover specials, designed to use up tortillas that are not fresh enough for other purposes. The tortillas are cut into strips or torn into small pieces and fried in oil until crisp. The pieces are combined with many kinds of foods and stir-cooked or baked.

Of course, at this point the fried tortillas are no longer crisp, but they have acquired a firm, meaty quality something like chicken. Because it offers the satisfaction of meat with mere scraps of leftover bread, Chilaquiles is sometimes called "Poor Man's Dish."

The Brunch or Almuerzo menu includes this dish (see page 19).

    6 corn tortillas
    3 tablespoons salad oil or butter
    ½ cup diced onion
    ¼ cup chopped canned California green chiles
    ½ teaspoon salt
    6 eggs
    1 cup shredded jack cheese or
        medium-sharp Cheddar cheese
        Red Chile Sauce (canned or made by
        recipe on page 21)

Cut the tortillas into strips about ³/₈ inch wide. Fry over medium heat in hot salad oil or butter, stirring, until crisp. Add the diced onion, chopped chiles, salt, and eggs, and mix well. Cook, stirring, until eggs are partially set. Sprinkle with shredded cheese and continue cooking, stirring, until eggs are cooked as you like. Top each serving with sauce. Serves 4.

Tortilla "Dry Soup"
SOPA SECA DE TORTILLAS (*soh*-pah *seh*-kah)

Because this spicy casserole, rich with cream and cheese, contains strips of tortillas, it might also be classified with Chilaquiles.

    12 corn tortillas, cut in thin strips
    ⅓ cup lard or shortening
    1 cup minced onion
    2 tablespoons lard or shortening
    4 canned California green chiles, seeded
        and minced
    1 cup whipping cream
    1 cup tomato purée
        Salt
    ½ pound shredded jack cheese
    2 tablespoons butter

Sauté tortillas in the ¹/₃ cup lard until crisp, but do not brown.

To make sauce, sauté onion in the 2 tablespoons lard until transparent; add chiles, cream, and tomato purée. Simmer 10 minutes; salt.

Grease a 2-quart baking dish and cover bottom with half the tortilla strips. Pour over half the sauce and add a layer of half the shredded cheese. Repeat layers, ending with cheese. Dot with butter and bake in a 350° oven for 30 minutes. Makes 6 servings.

Huevos Rancheros

(*weh*-vohs rrran-*che*-rohs)

These country-style eggs are more than just a dish; properly served they become a meal. Fried eggs are placed atop mildly sauced, lightly fried tortillas and garnished with buttery avocado. They invariably are accompanied by Refried Beans. (If you prefer, poach or scramble the eggs.)

2 medium-sized onions, finely chopped
1 tablespoon salad oil
1 can (10 oz.) Mexican red chile sauce
1 can (8 oz.) tomato sauce
½ teaspoon crumbled oregano
1 tablespoon butter
1 can (1 lb.) Refried Beans
½ cup shredded jack or Cheddar cheese
6 hot fried corn tortillas (directions follow)
6 or 12 fried eggs (directions follow)
12 avocado slices
    Canned or bottled salsa jalapeña or
        green chile salsa (sauce)

Cook onion in salad oil until soft; add red chile sauce, tomato sauce, and oregano. Bring to a full boil, then simmer gently, uncovered, for 15 minutes; stir occasionally. Use hot, or cool and reheat.

Cut butter in small pieces and mix with Refried Beans; spread in a small shallow casserole and sprinkle with cheese. Bake, uncovered, in a 350° oven for 15 minutes.

Dip each hot fried tortilla in heated sauce, coating both sides; then place tortillas on individual dishes, or side by side on a large tray. Spoon all the sauce evenly over tortillas and top each with 1 or 2 hot fried eggs. Garnish with avocado slices.

Pass salsa jalapeña (a hot sauce) or green chile salsa (a milder preparation) to be added as desired. Accompany with the hot Refried Beans. Makes 6 main-dish servings.

Fried Tortillas. Heat about ½ inch salad oil in a small frying pan over moderate heat. Fry tortillas, one at a time, until slightly crisp; turn frequently. Drain on paper towels. Keep warm for a few minutes on an electric warming tray or in the oven if you plan to serve at once; or let cool, then spread in a single layer on a baking sheet and bake at 350° (in the same oven where the beans are baking) for about 4 minutes.

Fried Eggs. Melt 2 tablespoons butter in a 10 to 12-inch frying pan over medium-low heat. Break 6 eggs into pan (use 2 pans for 12 eggs, or cook in succession). Sprinkle with about ¼ cup shredded jack cheese and 1 tablespoon water. Cover and cook until eggs are set the way you like; salt to taste and transfer onto sauce-coated tortillas.

Topopo

(toh-*poh*-poh)

A counterpart for our hearty chef's salad takes the much more dramatic shape of a mountain or volcano. This main-dish salad is typical of the cuisine shared by the northern state of Sonora with next-door Arizona and thus reflects tastes on both sides of the border.

2 whole corn tortillas, crisp-fried by directions
    on page 30
    About ½ cup hot, canned Refried Beans
    Topopo Salad (directions follow)
8 to 12 cold, cooked, shelled, deveined
    prawns, each cut in half lengthwise; or
    about 1 cup cold, sliced cooked turkey or
    chicken
1 avocado, pitted, peeled, and sliced
    lengthwise
    About ¼ cup diced longhorn or mild
    Cheddar cheese
1 canned California green chile, seeds and
    pith removed, then chopped
¼ cup shredded or grated Romano cheese
    Tomato wedges or canned *jalapeño* chiles

For each serving, spread tortilla with beans, covering completely. Place tortilla in a rimmed serving dish (about dinner plate size). Mound salad onto it to create a mountain shape.

Arrange shrimp, chicken, or turkey around the sides of the salad, then fill in with avocado slices. Sprinkle or place the pieces of cheese and California green chile over the salad. Spoon Romano cheese on the tip of the salad and top with tomato wedge or hot jalapeño chile. Serve at once. Makes 2 Topopos (2 main-dish servings).

Topopo Salad. Mix 1 cup cold cooked peas (or thawed frozen petit peas or drained canned peas) with 1 teaspoon minced jalapeño chile (seeds and pith removed), ½ cup chopped green onion, 4 to 5 cups finely shredded iceberg lettuce, ¼ cup salad oil, 2 tablespoons vinegar, and salt to taste.

VERSATILE ENCHILADAS

The filled tortilla favorites – rolled, folded, or stacked with an assortment of tasty embellishments

Other Mexican foods may rival the Enchilada in popularity, but few if any can equal it in sheer number of variations.

Mexican cooks have always been inventive, but for some reason Enchiladas have inspired them to the highest flights of fancy. An "authentic" Enchilada will have many versions, as the recipes in this chapter so aptly demonstrate. Suggestions even follow for ways you, too, can devise your own new recipes.

The first Enchiladas were probably made by the Indians in southern Mexico with corn tortillas. The Sonora type made with flour tortillas later appeared in northern Mexico when the tribes of that region began to grow the wheat introduced by Spaniards.

The ingredients of Enchiladas are tortillas, a sauce, a filling, and sometimes a garnish or topping (or both).

To make them, you dip tortillas in the sauce and fry briefly in oil. (Or to be neater but less traditional, fry tortillas and then dip in the sauce.) Then roll, fold, or stack them with fillings such as cheese, beans, or meat.

In Mexico, Enchiladas are served immediately after they are assembled. But the American way, geared to convenience, is to pour more sauce over the dish and bake just long enough to heat all the ingredients thoroughly. This means the Enchiladas can be assembled well ahead and reheated at the last minute.

Probably the greatest sins in Enchilada-making are to fry the tortillas so long that they become crisp or to bake the dish so long that the tortillas dry out and get crusty on the edges.

Much debate has centered on the subject of how chile-pepper-hot an Enchilada should be. The traditional sauce contains a blend of bland red chile pulp and spices, which give rich seasoning without piercing sharpness. But if you are among those who like the pleasant torture of throat-searing hotness, add hot chiles or liquid hot-pepper seasoning to the sauce, or select a pungent filling such as one made of chorizo sausages.

BASIC ENCHILADA STEPS

Here are the basic steps you will follow in making almost all kinds of Enchiladas:

Frying the Tortillas. Dip each tortilla into medium-hot shallow or deep fat. (Salad oil or shortening can be used, but Mexicans believe that lard gives best results.) Fry over medium heat just a few seconds, until it begins to blister and becomes limp—*do not fry until firm or crisp.* Remove with tongs or a pancake turner.
See first photo on page 38.

Saucing the Tortillas. As soon as you take the tortilla out of the hot fat, dip it into the heated sauce your recipe specifies. A cake pan just larger than the tortilla is ideal for holding sauce. (Mexican cooks reverse the procedure and dip the tortilla in sauce before frying it in oil, but this is so messy and splattery that most modernized recipes call for frying first.)
See second photo on page 38.

Filling and Shaping the Enchiladas. Lay the sauce-dipped tortilla out on a board or pan. Spoon the required amount of filling, warm or cold, in the center. (As the baking process will heat the filling through, it does not have to be hot, but it should not be icy cold.)

You may make Enchiladas in three forms— rolled, folded, or stacked. (Photo on page 41.)

For rolled ones, turn the tortilla over the filling, roll, and place with the flap pointing down in a baking pan or on a heatproof serving plate. Pour additional sauce over the panful of Enchiladas, enough to make a shallow layer of sauce in the bottom of the pan and to moisten the tortillas well so they will not dry out while baking.

For the folded kind, just turn the tortilla over the filling to make a half-moon shape and arrange neatly, slightly overlapping. Also pour additional sauce over these.

To make a "stack," spread the filling evenly over each tortilla and stack them in layers, spooning additional sauce between and on top of each layer. (When you serve, cut the stack into wedges.)

Garnishing and Baking Enchiladas. Some of the toppings are placed on before baking, such as shredded cheese, chopped onions, and olives. Place hard-cooked egg shreds or slices, avocado slices, slivered radishes, or sliced green onions on after baking.

Recipes vary, but a general rule for baking is to place the Enchiladas uncovered in a 350° oven for 15 to 20 minutes, or just until all is thoroughly heated. Before you bake, be sure the tortillas are well moistened with sauce all over so that they will not dry or crisp on the edges.

Serving Tips. Two or three Enchiladas usually make a serving. Traditionally the only accompaniments are Refried Beans and plain, hot tortillas, but most American Mexican restaurants also serve rice and a salad. Native cooks usually serve Enchiladas immediately after they are made; but for convenience you may fill and sauce them as much as eight hours ahead. In that case, pour a little more sauce over just before the baking, which should be done at serving time.

HOW TO VARY ENCHILADAS

Tortilla Variations. In addition to corn and flour tortillas, you may use the pancake-like Egg-Masa Tortilla (recipe on page 29) or a thin pancake of your own invention.

Sauce Variations. You can purchase canned Enchilada sauce or Mexican red chile sauce, as well as make a variety of sauces by recipes in this book.

Many Mexican cooks prefer a thinned *mole* sauce. Mole powder, made of a blend of spices, chiles, and ground chocolate (sometimes even ground nuts), is sold in little cans at Mexican and gourmet food shops. Prepare it according to label instructions and thin with broth or water to the right consistency. All Enchilada sauces should be creamy and pourable.

Other sauces can be based on the variety of canned tomato sauces now available, whipping or sour cream, canned green chile sauce, or other rich concoctions of your own invention.

Filling Variations. This list of filling ingredients already frequently used will give you an idea of the latitude you have in designing your own: ground or slivered cooked meat and poultry, shredded cheese, onions, Refried Beans, green chiles, hard-cooked eggs, Guacamole, sour cream. The filling should be moist but not runny. Sautéed onions or the sauce you use can be added to the filling for moisture. Raisins, nuts, olives, chopped vegetables, and many other tidbits can be added for flavor, color, and texture surprise.

Topping and Garnish Variations. An unlimited variety of garnishes can be added after the dish is baked, for flavor or appearance. In Texas, fried eggs are served on top, but poached eggs or slices of hard-cooked eggs could be used.

You could arrange borders of shredded or finely chopped raw vegetables and parsley, or sprinkle with these. Mushrooms, currants, toasted nuts, capers, pickled chile peppers (red, green, or yellow, hot or mild), salami cut in thin strips, crumbled bacon, or whatever your imagination comes up with could be decorative.

You might even design topping or sauce different from that used in the dish to serve in a bowl on the side.

ENCHILADA-MAKING begins with frying tortillas in hot fat, just long enough to soften them and make them puff.

SECOND STEP in making Enchiladas is coating the fried tortillas in a heated sauce; then you fill them.

Chicken Enchiladas, Uruápan

ENCHILADAS DE POLLO DE URUÁPAN
(*poh*-yoh theh oo-roo-*ah*-pan)

Cheese is the filling for the tortillas; chicken legs, simmered in a chile sauce until tender, are served on top. If you wish, you can cook the chicken ahead and refrigerate it in the sauce.

    6 to 8 whole broiler-fryer chicken legs
          (including thighs)
       Salt
    2 tablespoons salad oil
    1 small onion, finely chopped
    1 can (10 oz.) Mexican red chile sauce
    ¼ cup water
    12 corn tortillas
       Salad oil, shortening, or lard for
          frying tortillas
    ¾ cup grated Romano cheese
    2 cups shredded jack cheese
       Whole radishes, cucumber slices, and
          lime wedges for garnish

Sprinkle chicken pieces lightly with salt. Heat 2 tablespoons oil in a wide frying pan over medium-high heat and brown chicken well on all sides. Add onion, red chile sauce, and water, stirring to blend. Cover pan and simmer gently for about 30 minutes, or until chicken is tender. (At this point you can chill chicken in sauce as long as overnight, then reheat to simmering and continue.) Remove chicken from sauce and keep warm.

Fry tortillas in oil and dip into heated sauce (in which chicken was cooked) according to Basic Enchilada Steps on page 36. Stack tortillas as you go (they tear easily).

Mix Romano and jack cheese; spoon 2 generous tablespoons of cheese down center of each tortilla and fold in half over filling. Arrange Enchiladas, overlapping, on a heatproof serving platter or baking dish and place chicken alongside or on top. Spoon on remaining chicken sauce and sprinkle with balance of the cheese.

Bake uncovered in a 350° oven for 15 minutes to heat through. Garnish with radishes, cucumbers, and lime wedges. Squeeze lime onto individual servings. Makes 12 Enchiladas (4 to 6 servings).

Folded Pork Enchiladas

ENCHILADAS DE PUERCO DOBLADAS

(*puer*-koh thoh-*blah*-thas)

To make these, you just fold the tortillas over the filling instead of rolling. Otherwise, the procedure is the same as for the rolled kind.

```
16   corn tortillas
     Salad oil, shortening, or lard for frying
        tortillas
2½   cups Mexican Red Chile Sauce (canned
        or made by recipe on page 21)
 3   cups Pork Filling (recipe on page 24)
 ⅓   cup minced canned green chiles, seeds
        and pith removed
1½   cups shredded jack cheese
```

Fry tortillas in oil and dip into heated sauce according to Basic Enchilada Steps, page 36.

Spoon about 3 tablespoons Pork Filling and about 1 teaspoon minced chiles down the center of each; fold tortilla over filling to make a half-moon shape. Arrange Enchiladas, overlapping, in a shallow ungreased casserole.

Pour over enough sauce to make a shallow layer in the dish. Sprinkle with cheese. Bake uncovered in a 350° oven for 15 to 20 minutes or just until hot throughout. Serve with a bowl of the heated sauce. Makes 16 Enchiladas (5 to 8 servings).

Stacked Cheese Enchiladas

ENCHILADAS DE QUESO

(*keh*-soh)

You see this version in the northern state of Sonora. The tortillas are stacked, with a layer of filling covering each one, perhaps the easiest way to make Enchiladas.

```
10   corn tortillas
 1   cup Mexican Red Chile Sauce (canned or
        made by recipe on page 21)
     Salad oil, shortening, or lard for frying
        tortillas
 1   cup shredded sharp Cheddar cheese
 1   to 1½ cups chopped green onions
        (including some tops)
```

Fry tortillas in oil and dip into heated sauce according to Basic Enchilada Steps, page 36.

Place one tortilla in a small shallow ungreased casserole; spoon over the surface 1 or 2 tablespoons shredded sharp Cheddar, about 2 tablespoons chopped green onion, and a little of the remaining chile sauce. Add the remaining tortillas, preparing each layer the same way. Pour remaining sauce over the stack, and top with remaining cheese.

Bake uncovered in a 350° oven for 15 to 20 minutes, or until hot. Cut in wedges to serve. Serves 4 or 5.

Rolled Beef Enchiladas

ENCHILADAS DE RES ENROLLADAS

(rrres en-roh-*yah*-thas)

Sour cream, cool and smooth, is spooned onto baked Enchiladas for a pleasant flavor contrast. Red Chile Sauce you make yourself helps give this dish its special character, but you could substitute canned Mexican red chile or Enchilada sauce if you wish.

```
16   corn tortillas
     Salad oil, shortening, or lard for frying
        tortillas
     About 2½ cups Mexican Red Chile Sauce
        (canned or made by recipe on page 21)
 3   cups Ground Beef Filling (recipe on
        page 24)
 ¾   cup chopped onion
1½   cups shredded sharp Cheddar cheese
 2   cups (1 pint) sour cream
```

Fry tortillas in oil and dip into heated sauce according to Basic Enchilada Steps, page 36.

Spoon about 3 tablespoons Ground Beef Filling down the center of each tortilla, and sprinkle with about 2 teaspoons onion. Roll tortilla around filling and place, flap side down, in an ungreased shallow casserole. Place filled Enchiladas side by side.

Pour enough sauce over the Enchiladas to moisten entire surface of the casserole. Sprinkle with cheese. Bake uncovered in a 350° oven for 15 to 20 minutes, or just until hot throughout. Serve with chilled sour cream as a topping. Makes 16 Enchiladas (5 to 8 servings).

Sour Cream Enchiladas

ENCHILADAS DE JOCOQUE (hoh-*koh*-keh)

Sour cream both fills and garnishes these rich Enchiladas, which are assembled a bit differently from most—pairs of overlapped tortillas are filled and folded.

Those who do not care for spicy food will find this light and refreshing.

The Steak Jalisco Barbecue menu includes this dish (see page 19).

      2 cups (1 pint) sour cream
      1 cup chopped green onions
          (including some tops)
    ½ teaspoon ground cumin
      4 cups (about 1 lb.) shredded longhorn
          Cheddar cheese
    12 corn tortillas
          Salad oil, shortening, or lard for
          frying tortillas
      1 can (10 oz.) Enchilada sauce
          Sour cream and chopped green onions
          for garnish

Blend the 2 cups sour cream, 1 cup chopped onion, cumin, and 1 cup of the shredded cheese.

Fry tortillas in the oil and dip into the heated Enchilada sauce according to Basic Enchilada Steps on page 36.

In an ungreased casserole about 8 by 10 inches (or 9 by 9 inches), overlap two tortillas at one end of the pan, allowing part of the tortillas to extend over the edge of the pan. Spread about 6 tablespoons of the sour cream filling down the center of the tortillas, and fold the extending sections down over the filling.

Repeat this technique to fill remaining tortillas, placing them side by side and completely covering the pan bottom; use all the filling. Sprinkle the remaining 3 cups cheese evenly over the top. (You can cover and chill the casserole for 3 or 4 hours if you want to make it ahead.)

Bake uncovered in a 375° oven for 20 minutes. Garnish with more sour cream spooned down the center of the Enchiladas and sprinkle with more green onions. Makes 6 large Enchiladas (about 6 servings).

Chorizo Enchiladas

ENCHILADAS DE CHORIZO (cho-*ree*-soh)

In some parts of Mexico and the southwestern United States, chorizo refers not only to the spicy link sausage but also to a highly seasoned ground meat mixture sold fresh just as regular bulk sausage sometimes is. You make just such a chorizo mixture to fill these Enchiladas.

The longhorn cheese specified has better melting qualities than other Cheddars and more closely resembles cheese used in Mexico.

          Bulk Chorizo Sausage Filling
              (recipe on page 24)
    ¾ cup canned Enchilada sauce
    1½ cups *each* shredded jack and longhorn
              Cheddar cheese
    12 corn tortillas
          Salad oil, shortening, or lard for
          frying tortillas
      1 cup (½ pint) sour cream
          Pitted ripe olives for garnish
      1 can (about 8 oz.) frozen Guacamole,
          thawed (or about 1 cup made from
          recipe on page 21)

Prepare Bulk Chorizo Sausage Filling according to the recipe on page 24, using the amount of Enchilada sauce called for there. (One large can of the sauce—1 lb. 3 oz.—will provide enough both for making the filling and for supplying the ¾ cup specified in the ingredient list above.)

Cool the filling slightly and stir in ½ cup *each* of the jack and longhorn Cheddar cheeses.

THREE ENCHILADA SHAPES are possible—with the tortillas rolled (right), folded (left), or stacked (above) to enclose a filling. Varied garnishes may be baked on the dish or added just before serving.

Fry tortillas in oil and dip into the reserved ¾ cup heated Enchilada sauce according to Basic Enchilada Steps on page 36.

In a 9-inch-square, ungreased baking pan, overlap two tortillas to extend across one side of pan, allowing part of tortillas to extend over the rim. Spoon ⅙ of the meat mixture down center of tortillas and fold over the filling. Repeat this technique to fill remaining tortillas, placing them side by side, overlapping on unfilled edges until the pan is filled. Sprinkle top with the remaining cheese.

Bake casserole uncovered in a 350° oven for 30 minutes. Spoon on sour cream decoratively, top with olives, and serve with Guacamole as a sauce.

(You can assemble the casserole ahead, then cover and chill it as long as overnight. Bake chilled casserole for 50 minutes, keeping it covered for the first 20 minutes.) Makes 6 to 8 servings.

Sonora Enchiladas with Masa

ENCHILADAS DE SONORA CON MASA
(soh-*noh*-rah kon *mah*-sah)

The cheese filling is deep-fried right into the tortilla in this variation, made differently from most Enchiladas.

>   2 cups Masa Harina (dehydrated masa flour)
> 1⅓ cups warm water
>   3 tablespoons lard
>   1 teaspoon salt
>   About ½ cup grated Parmesan cheese
>   ¼ cup flour
>   Salad oil, shortening, or lard for frying
>   1 can (10 oz.) Enchilada or Mexican red
>   chile sauce

Mix thoroughly the masa flour and water. Stir in lard, salt, ¼ cup of the cheese, and flour. Form into round cakes about 5 inches in diameter and ¼ inch thick. Dip into remaining cheese to coat.

Drop into hot oil (about 375°) and fry until golden and crisp. Serve the flat cakes with chilled sauce to spoon over. Makes six 5-inch-diameter Enchiladas (3 servings).

Beef & Bean Enchiladas

ENCHILADAS DE RES Y FRIJOLES REFRITOS
(free-*hoh*-less rrreh-*free*-tohs)

You could serve these for a buffet meal, letting each person help himself to the sour cream and chile sauce toppings. If you wish, you can assemble the casserole and refrigerate it for several hours, or overnight, before baking.

    1½ pounds ground beef
     1 medium-sized onion, chopped
     1 can (1 lb.) Refried Beans
     1 teaspoon salt
     ⅛ teaspoon garlic powder
     ⅓ cup bottled or canned Taco sauce
     1 cup quartered, pitted ripe olives
    12 corn tortillas
        Salad oil, shortening, or lard for
          frying tortillas
     2 cans (10 oz. *each*) Enchilada sauce
     3 cups shredded Cheddar cheese
          (about 10 oz.)
        Sliced pitted ripe olives for garnish
        Sour cream
        Canned green chile salsa (sauce)

In a frying pan crumble ground beef and sauté with onions until meat is browned and onions are soft. Stir in beans, salt, garlic powder, Taco sauce, and olives; heat until bubbly.

Dip tortillas, one at a time, in hot oil to soften; drain quickly.

Heat Enchilada sauce; pour about half into an ungreased, shallow 3-quart baking dish.

Place about ⅓ cup of the ground beef filling on each tortilla, and roll to enclose filling. Place, flap side down, in the sauce in the bottom of the baking dish. Pour remaining Enchilada sauce evenly over tortillas; cover with cheese. Bake uncovered in a 350° oven for about 15 to 20 minutes, or until thoroughly heated.

(Or cover and refrigerate for up to 1 day; if taken directly from refrigerator, increase baking time to 45 minutes.)

Garnish with olive slices. Spoon sour cream and green chile sauce over each serving. Makes 12 Enchiladas (4 to 6 servings).

Swiss Enchiladas

ENCHILADAS SUIZAS (*swee*-sass)

Swiss Enchiladas, sauced in heavy cream, are named for a country where dairy products are more plentiful than in Mexico.

     2 cups chopped cooked chicken or turkey
     ½ can (4 oz. size) California green
          chiles, rinsed, seeds and pith removed,
          and minced
     1 can (7 oz.) green chile salsa (sauce)
     ½ teaspoon salt
     2 cups whipping cream
    12 corn tortillas
        Salad oil, shortening, or lard for
          frying tortillas
    1½ cups shredded jack cheese

Combine chicken, chiles, and chile sauce for filling. Mix salt with cream for sauce.

Fry each tortilla in medium-hot oil a few seconds, until it blisters and is limp, then dip into cream. Fill with chicken mixture. Roll and place in an ungreased baking pan, flap side down. When all tortillas are filled, pour remaining cream over them. Sprinkle with cheese.

Bake uncovered in a 350° oven for 15 to 20 minutes, or until thoroughly heated. Makes 12.

Meat-Raisin Enchiladas

ENCHILADAS DE PICADILLO (pee-kah-*thee*-yoh)

Raisins are a sweet accent in the meat filling for these Enchiladas. This filling is good with Egg-Masa Tortillas, sort of a cross between French pancakes and the usual tortillas.

        Warm water
     ¼ cup raisins
    1¾ cups finely diced cooked beef or pork
     ¼ cup minced onion
        About 2 cups Chile-Tomato Sauce
          (recipe on page 22)
    10 pitted ripe olives
    10 Egg-Masa Tortillas (recipe on page 29)
          or corn tortillas
        Salad oil, shortening, or lard for
          frying tortillas

Run warm water over raisins to plump them; drain. Mix with beef, onion, and ⅓ cup of the sauce.

Fry tortillas in oil and dip into heated sauce according to Basic Enchilada Steps, page 36.

Roll a spoonful of filling and an olive into each tortilla and arrange in a shallow ungreased baking dish. Pour enough of the sauce into the dish to make a shallow layer. Bake uncovered for 15 to 20 minutes in a 350° oven, or until heated through. Makes 10 Enchiladas (about 4 or 5 servings).

Souffléed Green Chile Enchilada

ENCHILADAS DE CHILE VERDE EN SOUFFLÉ
(*chee*-leh *ver*-deh)

Quite unlike a typical Enchilada, this casserole consists of a puffy egg mixture—resembling a soufflé, but more stable—baked in a tortilla-lined dish. The casserole goes well with simply roasted or grilled meats or poultry, or it can be a main dish for a light meal.

For a family supper, you may serve it with broiled ground beef patties, a simple green salad dressed with oil and vinegar, Mexican hot chocolate (recipe on page 93), and crisp cookies.

    7 or 8 corn tortillas
      Salad oil, shortening, or lard for
        frying tortillas
    1 can (7 oz.) green chile salsa (sauce)
    4 eggs, separated
    1 tablespoon flour
    1¾ cups shredded jack cheese
    3 to 4 canned California green chiles,
        rinsed, seeds and pith removed, and
        finely chopped
    1 mild pickled red pepper for garnish

Fry tortillas in oil and dip into heated sauce according to Basic Enchilada Steps, page 36.

Put 1 tortilla in the bottom of a 7 or 8-inch-diameter ungreased casserole (at least 2 inches deep); arrange the remaining tortillas, overlapping, around the sides and slightly over the bottom center tortilla.

Beat egg whites until stiff; set aside. With same beater whip egg yolks until slightly thickened, then beat in flour; stir in 1 cup of the cheese, the chiles (taste first to decide the amount of hot flavor you want, adding more or less as you like), and a little of the egg white. Fold yolk mixture into remaining whites and pour into tortilla-lined dish.

Fold tortillas down over filling. Spoon salsa (remaining after you have dipped tortillas) onto tortillas, then sprinkle evenly with remaining cheese.

Bake uncovered in a 375° oven for 30 minutes. Garnish with pepper and serve. Makes 6 side-dish servings or 4 main-dish servings.

Acapulco Enchiladas

ENCHILADAS DE ACAPULCO

Slivered almonds give a pleasing crunchiness to the rich filling of these Enchiladas, named for their place of origin.

    2 cups diced cooked chicken or turkey
    ½ cup chopped ripe olives
    1 cup slivered or coarsely chopped almonds
    3 cups canned Enchilada or Mexican Red
        Chile Sauce (canned or made by
        recipe on page 21)
    12 corn tortillas
      Salad oil, shortening, or lard for
        frying tortillas
    1½ cups shredded sharp Cheddar cheese
    2 cups (1 pint) sour cream
    4 tablespoons minced green onions

Make the filling by combining chicken, olives, almonds, and enough of the sauce to moisten (about ⅓ cup).

Fry tortillas in oil and dip into heated sauce according to Basic Enchilada Steps, page 36.

Spoon some of the chicken mixture along the center of each tortilla. Roll and place, flap side down, in a shallow ungreased baking dish. Top with remaining sauce and sprinkle with cheese.

Bake uncovered in a 350° oven for 15 to 20 minutes, or until heated through. Mix sour cream with onions and serve cold as a sauce. Makes 12 Enchiladas (4 to 6 servings).

TAMALES & ANTOJITOS

Corn masa specialties: Tamales, both meaty and sweet, and the snacks called "Little Whims"

Masa Harina, coarse flour made of specially prepared corn which is the basis for tortillas, also makes a variety of small edibles which may be served at any meal of the day or as snacks. The familiar Tamales are one group of these. Other types are called Antojitos ("little whims"), a word which implies tidbits or snacks and often also is applied to any kind of food eaten as a snack.

To make any of the Tamales or Antojitos in this chapter you must be able to obtain the Masa Harina, also called dehydrated masa flour. There are no substitutes which will give proper results.

The dehydrated masa flour is sold in bags at Mexican stores or other groceries specializing in foreign foods; you may even find it at supermarkets in areas of the West and Southwest which have a large Latin American population. For information about sources of supply, see the Masa and Masa Harina listing on page 10.

The doughs used for both Tamales and the Antojitos contains just three basic ingredients in varying proportions—the masa flour, liquid (water or broth), and lard. Lard is preferable for authentic texture and flavor. Salt and other seasonings may be added.

Tamales are most familiar in the United States in just one of their various forms—the meat-filled kind. However, there are some surprising sweet ones, also prepared in a corn-husk wrapper. Tamales de Frutas, of fruit, most often are made for a breakfast with eggs, ham, fresh fruit, and coffee. The caramel kind (Tamales de Dulces or Tamales de Caramelo) are usually served at *cena*, the light evening meal, sometimes at breakfast, and at any snack time.

The Antojitos consist of little fried masa-dough cakes in disc or boat shapes heaped with meat, beans, cheese, and other toppings. Each has a name, such as Sopes or Gorditas, which describes the shape. Several of these can make an entrée served on a plate to be eaten with a fork. Or they can be picked up to eat like a sandwich or an appetizer.

Immediately following are basic instructions for making all types of Tamales, plus recipes for the dough and fillings. Antojitos recipes are at the end of this chapter.

BASIC TAMALE PROCEDURE

All Tamales, whether sweet or meaty, have three main parts—a filling, a coating of masa dough around that, and an outside wrapper of corn husks or some other material to hold the whole concoction together while it is steam-cooked. (In some parts of Mexico, banana leaves are used.)

Variety is obtained by changes in the fillings and in ingredients or proportions of the masa dough.

Typical Mexican Tamales are smaller and flatter than those to which you may be accustomed. About 3 meat ones or 2 sweet ones will make a serving. You can also make them even smaller for cocktail-time; these little ones are called Tamalitos.

The Tamale-making procedure is briefly this: Spread a corn husk with the masa dough, put several spoonfuls of filling in the center, then fold the husk around the food to make a little packet. Stack the packets in a steamer and steam until the masa dough is cooked and firm. The step-by-step photographs on page 46 will show you just how easy this is. Tamale-making is also fun for a small group.

The following general directions (for preparing husks, folding Tamales, and steaming them) should be used in conjunction with each of the specific recipes in this chapter.

CORN HUSKS FOR TAMALES

You can purchase dried shucks in plastic bags or in bulk at many grocery and specialty food stores which handle Mexican foods.

You can also use fresh corn shucks. Many supermarkets strip them off before displaying corn and could save some at your request. However, American ears of corn which are smaller produce smaller husks. You will need to "patch" several together with masa dough as you make each Tamale.

(Note: The Mexican singular is Tamal, but Tamale has become the form used in the United States.)

Or dry your own by leaving the green shucks in a warm, sunny spot for 3 to 8 days or until yellow; store in a dry place.

If corn shucks are not available, you can use 6 by 8-inch pieces of foil, clear plastic wrap, polyethylene wrap for sandwiches, or parchment paper. However, these materials do not contribute the proper flavor, and the fact that they are nonporous causes the Tamales to taste dry.

One pound of dried husks will make about 100 Tamales.

To prepare, soak in warm water just until pliable; remove any silks or extraneous materials and wash shucks thoroughly. Don't worry about shucks that have split, as two small pieces can be overlapped and used as one. Cover the dry shucks with warm water and soak 2 hours to overnight. Keep damp until used.

FILLING & FOLDING TAMALES

For each Tamale select a wide, pliable, soaked corn husk. Lay husk flat on the working surface with tip away from you. *(Photo on next page.)*

For each Tamale, use 2 tablespoons Masa Dough for Meat Tamales (page 47); or use 1½ tablespoons Masa Dough for Fruit Tamales or Masa Dough for Caramel Tamales (page 48).

Spread dough on the husk, in a rectangle; the greater dimension should be across the width of the husk. This rectangle of masa should be placed so that it is completely to the right edge, with margins of 2 or 3 inches at the bottom, at least 1 inch at the left side, and at least 2 inches at the top (generally much more).

The rectangle of masa dough should be about 5 by 4 inches for meat Tamales, smaller for fruit or caramel ones (about 4 x 3½ inches).

If the husk is not wide enough to provide for a rectangle of dough this size with ample margins, use some masa dough to paste a piece of husk on to the back of it.

Spoon 2 tablespoons meat, 2 teaspoons fruit, or 1½ teaspoons caramel filling into the center of the masa strip. To enclose, turn the right side over to the center of the filling; then fold the left side over filling, allowing the plain part of the husk to wrap around the Tamale. Fold the bottom end over the mound of dough-enclosed filling, then fold down the tip of the husk, wrapping it around the Tamale if it is long enough. Lay fold-side down to hold it shut. If necessary, you can tie it with a strip of thick husk about ¼ inch wide. *See photo on next page.*

Tamales may be made in other shapes, but this simple one is most typically Mexican.

Tamalitos. All Tamales may be made in small size. Serve the meat ones as appetizers (you may want to add a few chopped canned California green chiles to the filling).

Shape just as you would regular Tamales, by the preceding instructions. The corn husks should be about ⅔ the regular size; trim large ones with scissors if necessary. For each Tamalito, use 1 tablespoon of masa dough for the type of Tamales you are making; spread in a 3½ by 2½-inch rectangle, and use 1 tablespoon meat, 1 teaspoon fruit, or 1 teaspoon caramel filling. Tamalitos require almost as much cooking time as regular Tamales.

TAMALE-MAKING begins with spreading masa dough in a rectangle to right edge of a pliable, presoaked corn husk.

FOLD right side of husk, coated to edge with masa, half over filling; fold left side over so masa edges meet.

FOLD bottom edge over center, then fold down tip of husk. Lay Tamale on tip to hold shut, or tie with husk strip.

TO STEAM, stack Tamales in deep pot on a rack placed well above boiling water; arrange so steam circulates, cover.

HOW TO STEAM TAMALES

Once the Tamales are folded, they are ready to steam. You can use a kettle designed for steaming or improvise one several ways. All you need is a rack placed above about 2 inches of water (which will be boiling) and a lid or cover to the container.

Use any large kettle or roasting pan. For the rack you can use a metal roasting, pressure cooker, or cake rack. Or make one from hardware cloth. Rest the rack on tin cans of equal height with both ends removed. Be sure the rack is well above the water so that it will not splash up onto the Tamales while boiling.

To steam, stack the Tamales on the rack, folded side down, arranging them loosely enough so that steam can circulate freely. Cover the kettle and place over medium heat so that the water will boil gently. *See photo on opposite page.*

The cooking time will vary according to the number of Tamales you have stacked in the steamer, but will usually be about 45 minutes to 1 hour. To test for doneness, remove a Tamale from the top and one from the center of the stack. Open them; they are done if the masa dough is firm, does not stick to the shuck, and does not have a raw, doughy taste.

You may freeze cooked Tamales; to reheat (unthawed), steam them about 20 to 30 minutes, or until thoroughly hot throughout.

To wrap Tamales for freezing, arrange a stack of about 6 on a rectangle of clear plastic wrap or foil. Wrap securely and seal with tape on which you record the date and type of Tamale. For best quality, use within 6 weeks.

Masa Dough for Meat Tamales

MASA PARA TAMALES DE RES
(*mah*-sah *pah*-rah tah-*mah*-less deh rrres)

If you need double or triple the quantity of dough yielded by this recipe, still make batches with about 4 cups masa flour at a time. The dough is very difficult to mix in large quantity.

1⅓ cups (⅔ lb.) lard
4 cups Masa Harina (dehydrated masa flour)
2 teaspoons salt
2⅔ cups warm water *or* meat or poultry broth

Whip the lard until fluffy. Blend in the masa flour, salt, and warm water or broth until the dough holds together well.

Cover with a damp cloth and keep cool until ready to use. Makes 6 cups, or enough for 40 regular-sized Tamales (each using 2 tablespoons of prepared masa).

Fillings for Meat Tamales

RELLENOS PARA TAMALES (rrreh-*yeh*-nohs)

You may use either of two basic filling recipes: Beef Filling and Pork or Chicken Filling (this may also be made with turkey), both on page 24.

Either of these two recipes makes about 3 cups of filling, enough for only about 20 Tamales. The Masa Dough for Meat Tamales recipe preceding will make 40 Tamales; therefore, you need to double either of the filling recipes to have enough to match that quantity of masa dough.

If you make as many as 200 Tamales, an 18 to 20-pound turkey will supply enough meat and at the lowest cost. You can first roast the bird to get the meat, then simmer the bones to make a stock which can be used for flavor in making the masa dough.

Follow the basic Tamale-making instructions on pages 44-47 for using whatever filling you choose with prepared Masa Dough for Meat Tamales.

After you have steamed the Tamales according to the basic instructions, you might like to serve them with a sauce, even though this is not usually done in Mexico. You may heat either canned Mexican red chile sauce or homemade Red Chile Sauce (page 21). Canned Enchilada sauce also would be suitable. Another easy and delicious sauce may be made from Mexican *mole* powder, which comes in 3-ounce cans. Simmer the powder with 1½ cups chicken or beef stock; serve hot.

Masa Dough for Caramel Tamales
MASA PARA TAMALES DULCES (*dool*-sehs)

The brown sugar in this dough will make a richer-colored, sweeter Caramel Tamale. You may also use the plain Masa Dough for Meat Tamales (page 47), made with water rather than broth.

>   1 cup (½ lb.) lard
>   3 cups Masa Harina (dehydrated masa flour)
> 1½ cups water
>   ⅔ cup dark brown sugar
>   1 teaspoon salt
> 1½ teaspoons baking powder

Beat the lard until fluffy with an electric mixer. Blend in the masa flour, water, brown sugar, salt, and baking powder.

For each Tamale, spread about 1½ tablespoonfuls of this mixture on a prepared corn shuck according to methods described in general directions on page 45 and photographs on page 46. This will make about 40 Tamales.

Filling for Caramel Tamales
RELLENO PARA TAMALES DULCES

Add either raisins or nuts to this sweet caramel filling for Tamales.

>   2 cups dark brown sugar, firmly packed
>   ½ cup (¼ lb.) soft butter or lard
>   ¾ cup raisins, chopped walnuts,
>   pine nuts, *or* almonds

Blend the brown sugar with butter or lard. Stir in *either* the walnuts, raisins, pine nuts, or almonds. For each Tamale, use about 1½ teaspoons of this mixture. Makes enough for 40 Tamales.

These are best served hot, but may be eaten at room temperature. They may be reheated by steaming—see instructions on page 47.

Masa Dough for Fruit Tamales
MASA PARA TAMALES DE FRUTAS (*fru*-tahs)

You can combine fruit flavors by using the purée of one fruit in the masa dough and using another fruit in the filling.

>   1 cup (½ lb.) lard
>   3 cups Masa Harina (dehydrated masa flour)
>   Canned peaches, pineapple, or apricots,
>   puréed to make 1¼ cups
>   ½ cup sugar
>   1 teaspoon salt
> 1½ teaspoons baking powder
>   About 2 tablespoons juice from the
>   canned fruit if dough is too stiff to
>   spread easily

Whip lard with an electric mixer until light and fluffy. Blend in the masa flour, fruit purée, sugar, salt, baking powder, and fruit juice if necessary.

For each Tamale, spread about 1½ tablespoonfuls of this mixture on a prepared corn shuck according to methods described in general directions on page 45 and photographs on page 46. This will make about 40 Tamales.

Fillings for Fruit Tamales
RELLENOS PARA TAMALES DE FRUTAS

You may use either fresh fruit, preserves, or jam to fill Fruit Tamales.

If you use fresh fruit (peaches, pineapple, cherries, or bananas), dice fruit and add about ¼ cup sugar for each cup of diced fruit. Use about 2 teaspoons of sweetened fruit for each Tamale.

If you use preserves or jam (strawberry, apricot, or pineapple), use about 2 teaspoons for each.

Here are some fruit combinations you might try. Fill peach purée masa dough with fresh cherries or banana, or with preserves of strawberry, apricot, or pineapple. Fill apricot purée masa dough with fresh peaches or pineapple, or with strawberry preserves. Fill pineapple purée masa dough with fresh banana, peaches, or cherries, or with strawberry or apricot jam.

The Masa Dough for Fruit Tamales recipe will make about 40 Tamales; you will need about 2 cups of fruit or jam to fill this many.

Masa Dough for Antojitos

MASA PARA ANTOJITOS (ahn-toh-*hee*-tohs)

This dough can be used for making four kinds of Antojitos for which recipes follow in this chapter—Gorditas, Sopes, Garnaches, and Chalupas. *See photos on the next page.*

Each cup of this dough (the recipe makes more than 5 cups) will make the following quantities of *each* kind: 24 little Sopes, 10 Gorditas, 5 large Garnaches, or 8 Chalupas.

For all these, the dough is formed into cakes which are then fried in oil. You top the cakes with the fillings and garnishes specified in the recipes, which are immediately following.

This dough keeps several days refrigerated (wrap well so that it does not dry out); it also may be frozen.

```
4   cups Masa Harina (dehydrated masa flour)
2⅔  cups warm water or meat or poultry broth
⅔   cup (⅓ lb.) lard
2   teaspoons salt
```

Mix masa flour with the warm water or broth until the dough holds together well. Whip lard or shortening until fluffy. Beat in the masa and the salt. Cover with a damp cloth and keep cool until ready to use. Makes about 5½ cups.

Gorditas

(gohr-*dee*-tahs)

Gorditas means "little fat ones," an appropriate name for these plump, calorie-laden snacks.

If you prefer the chorizo sausage filling for these to be less highly seasoned, use half sausage and half ground beef.

```
1   cup Masa Dough for Antojitos
      (recipe above)
    Salad oil, shortening, or lard for frying
    About ½ pound chorizo sausages
¾   cup shredded lettuce
¼   cup shredded jack cheese
2   tablespoons chopped onion
```

For each Gordita base, shape about 1½ tablespoons of the Masa Dough for Antojitos into a flat round cake 4 inches in diameter.

GORDITA bases of masa, shaped with a rim, are fried in oil. Spoon fat inside to cook centers; do not turn.

Bake on a medium-hot ungreased griddle or frying pan over medium-high heat, turning occasionally, until masa begins to lose its doughy look. Remove cake from heat and let cool until you can touch it. With your fingers, pinch a slight ridge around the edge of the cake to form a very shallow cup. You can do this ahead. *See photograph above.*

Fry in about ½ inch hot oil over medium heat until lightly browned. Do not turn; ladle hot fat into cake to cook top. Drain on paper towels.

Remove casings from sausages, crumble the meat, and brown it in a frying pan. Drain off excess fat. Fill each base with about 1½ tablespoons of the meat. Sprinkle each with about 1 tablespoon lettuce, 2 teaspoons cheese, and about ½ teaspoon onion. Makes 10 Gorditas.

Completed Gorditas are shown at the bottom of the photograph on the next page.

ANTOJITOS in four shapes are (from top): Garnaches, boat-shaped Chalupas, tiny Sopes, and Gorditas.

Sopes

(*so*-pehs)

These are the quickest Antojitos to make if you use canned Refried Beans. You can even eliminate the step of baking the dough cakes on a griddle if you wish; just fry them in the oil. Lard will give the best flavor and flakiest results.

See photograph in left column.

1 cup Masa Dough for Antojitos
   (recipe on page 49)
   Salad oil, shortening, or lard for frying
1 cup Refried Beans (canned or made by
   recipe on page 22)
½ cup shredded sharp Cheddar cheese
6 radishes, sliced in fourths

For each Sope base, shape 2 teaspoons of the masa dough in a ball and pat into a flat round cake 2 to 2½ inches in diameter. Bake on a medium-hot ungreased griddle or heavy frying pan over medium-high heat, turning occasionally, until masa is dry looking and Sope is flecked with brown. You can do this ahead.

Fry Sope, turning, in ¼ inch hot oil over medium heat until lightly browned. Drain on paper towels, then top each cake with about 2 teaspoons hot beans, about 1 teaspoon shredded cheese, and a radish slice. Makes 24 Sopes.

Garnaches

(gahr-*nah*-chehs)

These are just a little too large to pick up and eat out of hand comfortably. If you want to serve them as appetizers, make them half-size.

See photograph in left column.

1 cup Masa Dough for Antojitos
   (recipe on page 49)
   Salad oil, shortening, or lard for frying
1 to 1¼ cups Ground Beef Filling (page 24)
   or Pork or Chicken Filling (page 24)
6 tablespoons shredded sharp Cheddar cheese
   Onion rings and hot pickled chiles
    for garnish

For each one, shape about 3 tablespoons of the Masa Dough for Antojitos into a round cake about 5 inches in diameter.

Bake on a medium-hot ungreased griddle or frying pan over medium-high heat, turning occasionally, until masa begins to lose its doughy look. Remove cake from heat and let cool until you can touch it. Then pinch up edge with your fingers to make a rim about 1/2 inch high.

Fry in about 1/2 inch hot oil until lightly browned. Do not turn; ladle hot fat into cake to cook top. Drain on paper towels.

Fill each with 3 or 4 tablespoons meat filling, then sprinkle each with about 1 tablespoon shredded cheese. Garnish with onion rings and pickled chiles. Makes 5 Garnaches.

Chalupas

(cha-*loo*-pahs)

Chalupas, meaning "little boats," are named after the boats in the floating gardens of Xochimilco, one of the great attractions now for tourists.

See photograph on opposite page.

1 cup Masa Dough for Antojitos
   (recipe on page 49)
   Salad oil, shortening, or lard for frying
1 cup shredded or thinly sliced cooked
   pork or chicken
1/2 to 1 cup Fresh Tomato and Green Chile
   Sauce (recipe on page 20)
6 tablespoons grated Romano cheese

For each Chalupa, pat about 2 tablespoons of the Masa Dough for Antojitos into an oval-shaped cake about 4 inches long.

Bake on a medium-hot ungreased griddle or frying pan over medium-high heat, turning occasionally, until masa begins to lose its doughy look. Remove cake from heat and let cool until you can touch it. Then pinch edge with your fingers to make a rim.

Fry in about 1/2 inch hot oil until lightly browned. Do not turn; ladle hot fat into cake to cook top. Drain on paper towels.

Fill each cake with about 2 tablespoons meat and top with 1 or 2 tablespoons sauce. Sprinkle each with about 2 teaspoons cheese. Makes 8 Chalupas.

Chonitas

(choh-*nee*-tahs)

Chonitas, made in the old town of Alamos, Mexico, are named for an excellent cook, Chona, who originated the dish. Easy to prepare, Chonitas are masa-dough turnovers containing a mild pimiento-seasoned chicken filling and topped with a spicy sauce of tomatoes and chiles.

1 1/2 cups Masa Harina (dehydrated masa flour)
2/3 cup quick-cooking cracked wheat (bulgur)
1/2 cup grated Parmesan cheese
1/2 teaspoon salt
1/4 cup butter
   About 1 1/4 cups warm water
   Chicken-Pimiento Filling (recipe follows)
   Salad oil, shortening, or lard for deep frying
   Spicy Chile Sauce (recipe follows)

Mix thoroughly the masa flour, cracked wheat, Parmesan, and salt. Cut butter into small pieces and add. Thoroughly stir in enough warm water to make a soft dough that holds together. Form dough into about 8 round cakes, each about 4 1/2 inches in diameter and 1/4 inch thick. (For easiest handling, press out on waxed paper or aluminum foil.) Place about 2 tablespoons Chicken-Pimiento Filling (recipe below) in center of each cake; fold dough circle over, turnover style, to make half-circle; press edges together to seal.

Slip into 3/4 inch of hot fat (heated to about 370°) in frying pan. Fry Chonitas until golden brown on bottom, basting the top continually with the hot fat; turn and brown second side. Drain a moment on absorbent paper. Serve with Spicy Chile Sauce. Makes 8 Chonitas, about 4 servings.

Chicken-Pimiento Filling. Sauté 1/2 cup sliced green onion (white part only) in 2 tablespoons melted butter just until limp. Add and toss together thoroughly 1 cup finely diced cooked chicken, 1/4 cup grated Parmesan cheese, and 2 tablespoons finely minced pimiento.

Spicy Chile Sauce. Combine in a saucepan and cook over medium heat for about 5 minutes 1 can (8 oz.) Spanish-style tomato sauce; 1/2 cup water; 1/2 cup sliced green onion; 2 canned California green chiles, minced; and 1/2 teaspoon crumbled oregano.

MAIN-DISH SPECIALTIES

Typical dishes of meat, seafood, or dairy products

In the United States, nearly every Mexican restaurant menu has the same entrée reading: Tacos, Tostadas, Tamales, Enchiladas, and Chiles Rellenos. As a result, most Americans who travel to Mexico are surprised at the kinds of main dishes served.

The most surprising aspect of the typical dishes is their plainness. Broiled or roasted meats and poultry are popular, usually very simply seasoned or sauced.

Another surprise is the variety of seafood, also usually prepared plainly. Actually, it is perfectly natural that seafood would abound in a country which borders more on the sea than on land. The many streams and lakes provide freshwater fish as well.

Some of the recipes in this chapter reflect this love for plain meat and seafood, but each has some twist in seasoning or ingredient which makes it typically Mexican and unique enough to be intriguing to guests.

You also will find recipes for some of the main dishes more widely known to be Mexican, such as Turkey Mole, several kinds of stuffed peppers (Chiles Rellenos), chicken with rice (Arroz con Pollo), and Paella.

Some recipes for typical sandwiches, made with bread rather than with tortillas, and recipes for omelets are included for light meals.

No recipe is printed here for typical Chile con Carne, because American cook books abound with good versions of this old stand-by. Instead, a recipe is included for another kind of popular "chile with meat," Chile Verde, made with several kinds of green peppers and spices.

If you want to make your favorite Chile con Carne recipe the Mexican way, just use meat cut in chunks (stew meat) instead of the ground kind. Some food writers have said that Chile con Carne should not be made with tomatoes or that beans should not be added.

Ignore such advice if you choose. The Mexican cuisine has no rigid rules for anything. Serve American canned chile with beans at your Mexican-style meals if you wish, whatever the misinformed purists may say. It's a good main dish or soup, compatible with many Mexican foods.

If you prefer plain broiled steak, roast chicken, or fried fish rather than more complicated entrées, add other Mexican specialties to accompany it. You will still be serving just as authentic a meal.

Torta Sandwiches
TORTAS (tor-tas)

Mexico City abounds with shops selling sandwiches called Tortas, rolls filled with combinations of meats, cheese, and relishes similar to those used in Tacos. The roll used there is a *telera,* hard-crusted but soft in the middle; you can use a small French dinner roll. Serve Tortas warm, accompanied by crisp raw vegetables, corn chips, and iced tea, limeade, or beer.

    6 small French dinner rolls
          (about 3 or 4 inches long)
          Butter or margarine
    6 slices Canadian-style bacon, cut about
          ¼ inch thick
    ½ medium-sized avocado
    ¼ teaspoon salt
 1½ teaspoons lime juice
    6 slices jack cheese
          About ½ cup shredded lettuce
    2 teaspoons bottled red or green
          salsa jalapeña

Split dinner rolls. Spread cut sides of rolls with butter or margarine; grill buttered sides until lightly browned. Sauté bacon until lightly browned on each side. Cover bottom halves of rolls with bacon slices. Mash together avocado pulp, salt, and lime juice. Complete sandwiches by topping with jack cheese, avocado mixture, shredded lettuce, chile sauce, and tops of rolls. Serve immediately. Makes 6 sandwiches.

Chile & Cheese Sandwich

CHILES CON QUESO SECO
(*chee*-lehs kohn *keh*-soh *seh*-koh)

This spicy-sweet chile and cheese combination served on French bread makes an unusual open-faced sandwich or appetizer. The Mexicans call it Chiles con Queso Seco or "chiles with dry cheese" because you use grated "dry" (hard) cheese. The resulting mixture is very moist nevertheless. You can prepare the cheese mixture or even assemble the sandwiches in advance, but in either case the cheese needs to be kept refrigerated.

Summer Buffet menu includes this dish (see page 16).

    8 large, dry, mild red *pasilla*, *ancho*, or
         California chiles (4 to 5 oz.)
    ½ cup olive oil or salad oil
    ¼ cup wine vinegar
    2 tablespoons brown sugar
    5 whole black peppers
    5 whole cloves
    2 bay leaves
    1 pound dry jack cheese or
         Parmesan cheese, grated
       Paprika
       French bread

Wash chiles and place in a saucepan with ½ inch water; cover and simmer gently for about 5 minutes. Pull out seeds under running water. Drain and dry chiles on toweling.

Place in the bottom of a shallow casserole; cover with mixture of oil, vinegar, brown sugar, peppercorns, cloves, and bay leaves. Cover; leave about 8 hours or overnight at room temperature.

Remove and drain the chiles; cut in half and set aside. Discard peppercorns, cloves, and bay leaves; stir oil mixture into grated cheese. To assemble, cover each chile half with about a ¹/₃-inch layer of the cheese mixture, sprinkle with paprika, and serve on slices of French bread. Makes 8 servings.

"Little Joe" Steak Sandwich

EL PEPITO (ehl peh-*pee*-toh)

From Guadalajara comes this version of the steak sandwich known as El Pepito, or "Little Joe." Hot cooked steak, thinly sliced, is served on a crisp roll spread with avocado sauce and Refried Beans. Chile or Taco sauce takes the place of catsup or steak sauce.

    About 1 pound lean tender steak (such as
         sirloin, New York cut, or top round), cut
         1 inch thick and broiled or barbecued
    4 crusty round or rectangular rolls
         (each 3 to 4 inches long)
       Refried Beans with Cheese (directions follow)
       About ¼ cup Guacamole, homemade
         (recipe on page 21) or frozen (thawed)
    4 thin slices mild onion
       Canned Mexican red chile or Taco sauce

Trim any fat or gristle from steak and slice meat thinly across the grain. Split the rolls and spread one side of each with about 1 tablespoon of the Refried Beans and the other side with about 1 tablespoon of the Guacamole.

Pile an equal portion of steak on the bean side of each roll; put the onion slice on the Guacamole side. Serve the sandwiches open so that sauce can be added according to taste before they are closed. Eat the sandwiches out of hand or with a knife and fork. Makes 4 servings.

Refried Beans with Cheese. Heat about ¼ cup canned Refried Beans (or homemade from recipe on page 22) with 2 tablespoons shredded Cheddar cheese (mild or sharp) or jack cheese and 1 teaspoon butter or margarine. Spread on sandwiches while hot.

CHILES RELLENOS are made by stuffing chiles with cheese (above) or meat, then coating in batter and frying.

OMELET-LIKE coating (No. 3) works best if you mound batter in pan, add chile, and spoon more batter on top.

PUFFY COATING (No. 2) requires that chiles be dipped in batter, placed on saucer, and slid into cooking oil.

STUFFED CHILES (Chiles Rellenos) are often topped with tomato sauce and accompanied by rice and Refried Beans.

Chiles Rellenos
(chee-lehs rrreh-yeh-nohs)

Chiles Rellenos or "stuffed peppers" are one of the best-known dishes served by Mexican restaurants in America. Usually these are stuffed with cheese to make Chiles Rellenos con Queso. But in Mexico many kinds of meat, seafood, and bean fillings also are used. With this recipe you can make the cheese version or another kind, Chiles Rellenos con Picadillo, peppers stuffed with a spicy ground beef mixture called Picadillo.

To make Chiles Rellenos, you stuff the peppers, cover them with an egg batter, and fry. Here you have a choice of three batters, which will produce different kinds of coatings—thin and crispy, puffy, or omelet-like.

1 can (7 oz.) California green chiles *or*
    6 to 8 fresh California green chiles, peeled
    according to instructions on page 14
Cheese Filling *or* Picadillo Filling
    (recipes follow)
About ½ cup flour
Coating 1, 2, or 3 (recipes follow)
Salad oil for frying
Salsa de Jitomate (recipe follows), optional
Garnish of shredded jack cheese or
    sliced green onion tops, optional

Drain canned chiles, rinse, and cut a slit down the side of each; gently remove seeds and pith inside. Prepare fresh chiles, if used, according to instructions.

Stuff chiles with either type of filling; slightly lap the cut edges to hold the filling inside. Have flour ready in a shallow pan. Roll each chile in flour to coat all over, gently shake off excess.

Prepare one of the following coatings (batters) just before you want to fry the chiles. Coat and fry the chiles according to the instructions with each coating recipe.

If you like, top with hot Salsa de Jitomate and garnish with cheese or onion; or use a canned or homemade red chile sauce. Some people prefer Chiles Rellenos without sauce, particularly those with the thin, crispy coating. Makes 3 or 4 servings.

Cheese Filling. Use ½ pound jack cheese. Just stuff each chile with a piece of cheese about ½ inch wide, ½ inch thick, and 1 inch shorter than the chile. *See first photo on opposite page.*

Picadillo Filling. Lightly toast ¼ cup slivered almonds in 1 tablespoon butter in a frying pan; remove almonds. Brown ½ pound lean ground beef in the remaining butter. Add 1 minced clove garlic, ¼ cup tomato purée, ¼ cup seedless raisins, 2 tablespoons Sherry, 1 teaspoon cinnamon, ½ teaspoon salt, ¼ teaspoon ground cloves, 1 tablespoon vinegar, 1½ teaspoons sugar, and the almonds. Cook uncovered over medium heat for 20 minutes, or until most of the liquid has evaporated. Cool. Fill each chile with about 2 tablespoons of the filling.

Coating 1 (Thin and Crispy). Separate 5 eggs. Beat the egg whites with 1 teaspoon salt until they hold firm, soft peaks. Using the same beater, or a whip, beat egg yolks until thick; fold yolks into whites and use immediately.

Heat about ¼ inch salad oil in a wide frying pan over medium heat. Coat the chile all over with the egg batter and use two forks to remove from the batter. (If fresh chiles are used, hold each by its stem and just dip into the batter—canned chiles have no such handy stems.)

Fry in the hot oil just as many at one time as can be done without crowding. When each is golden brown on one side, turn over with a spatula and fork (or two spatulas) and fry until golden on the other side. Remove and drain briefly on paper towels. Serve immediately.

Coating 2 (Puffy). Separate 3 eggs. Beat the whites until they form soft peaks. Beat yolks with 1 tablespoon water, 3 tablespoons flour, and ¼ teaspoon salt until thick and creamy; fold into whites.

Heat about 1½ inches of oil in a wide frying pan over medium heat. Dip stuffed chiles into the fluffy batter, place on a saucer, and slide into the hot oil. When the bottoms are golden brown, gently turn using a spatula and fork, and cook other side—3 to 4 minutes per side. Drain on paper towels. *See photo on opposite page.*

Coating 3 (Omelet-Like). Separate 4 eggs. Beat the whites until they form soft peaks. Beat the egg yolks with 4 tablespoons flour, 1 tablespoon water, and ¼ teaspoon salt. Fold into whites.

In a buttered omelet pan or frying pan over medium heat, make an oval mound of about ½ cup of the mixture. (You can cook singly in a small omelet pan or 2 or 3 at a time in a large frying pan.) Quickly lay a stuffed chile in the center of the mound and spoon about ⅓ cup mixture over the top to encase the chile. *See photo on page 54.* Cook 2 to 3 minutes over medium-low heat; gently turn and cook 2 to 3 minutes longer, or until golden.

Salsa de Jitomate (Tomato Sauce). Sauté 3 tablespoons finely chopped onion and 1 minced clove of garlic in 1 tablespoon butter until golden. Stir in 1 can (15 oz.) Spanish-style tomato sauce, ⅓ cup water, ¼ teaspoon salt, and ¼ teaspoon crumbled oregano. Simmer for 15 minutes. Serve hot. Makes 2½ cups.

Chiles Stuffed with Beans

CHILES RELLENOS CON FRIJOLES

(kohn free-*hoh*-less)

Because cheese-stuffed chiles are so popular, we may take for granted that Chilles Rellenos are always stuffed with cheese. The Mexicans, however, sometimes fill them with meat, seafood, or beans.

Also, stuffed chiles are not always coated in batter and fried. Here they are baked with tomato and cheese topping.

½ cup minced onion
1 clove garlic, minced or mashed
2 tablespoons bacon fat or lard
1 can (1 lb.) kidney beans
   Salt
   Ground cumin
2 cans (4 oz. *each*) California green chiles, rinsed, seeded, and pith removed
2 tomatoes, peeled and sliced
1 tablespoon olive oil
1 cup shredded Cheddar cheese

Cook onion and garlic in bacon fat or lard until wilted. Drain kidney beans and add. Mash well and heat, seasoning with salt and cumin to taste.

Stuff the chiles with this mixture and arrange them in a baking dish. Cover with sliced tomatoes. Drizzle olive oil over the tomatoes, sprinkle with shredded cheese, and heat in a 350° oven for 15 minutes, or until the cheese is melted and lightly browned. Serve at once. Makes 8 servings.

Chile Verde

(chee-leh ver-deh)

Verde means "green" in Spanish. The *verde* in this meaty stew is supplied by both fresh bell pepper and canned California green chiles, plus chopped parsley. Make this dish ahead and reheat it at mealtime if you like. Serve it in bowls or as a sauce over rice.

1½ pounds *each* boneless beef chuck and boneless, lean pork shoulder, cut in 1-inch cubes
3 tablespoons olive oil or salad oil
1 medium-sized green bell pepper, seeded and coarsely chopped
1 large clove garlic, minced or mashed
2 large cans (1 lb. 12 oz. *each*) tomatoes
1 large can (7 oz.) California green chiles, seeded and chopped
⅓ cup chopped parsley
½ teaspoon sugar
¼ teaspoon ground cloves
2 teaspoons ground cumin, *or* 1 tablespoon whole cumin seed, crushed
1 cup dry red wine, *or* ¼ cup lemon juice and ¾ cup beef broth
   Salt

Brown about a quarter of the meat at a time on all sides in heated oil; remove with a slotted spoon and reserve. In pan drippings sauté bell pepper and garlic until soft; add a little more oil, if needed. In a large pan (at least 5 quarts) combine tomatoes and their liquid, green chiles, parsley, seasonings, and wine. Bring tomato mixture to a boil, then reduce heat to a simmer. Add browned meats, their juices, and sautéed vegetables. Cover and simmer for 2 hours, stirring occasionally.

Remove cover; simmer for about 45 minutes more until sauce is reduced to thickness you wish and meat is very tender. Taste and add salt. Makes 6 to 8 servings.

Stuffed Chiles with Walnuts

CHILES EN NOGADA (ehn noh-*gah*-tha)

Because the colors of the Mexican flag are echoed in the green chiles, the white sauce, and the red pomegranate seeds, this exotic dish, has become a favorite throughout the country on Independence Day, September 15. Its Spanish name means "chiles in walnut sauce."

    2 7-oz. cans or about 12 fresh California
          green chiles
    1 medium-sized onion, chopped
 1½ tablespoons melted shortening
    1 cup diced, cooked pork
    1 large tomato, peeled, seeded,
          and diced
    1 large apple, peeled and chopped
    1 pear, peeled and diced
    1 banana, diced
   ¼ cup chopped walnuts
    1 small clove garlic, minced or mashed
   ¼ teaspoon salt, or more to taste
       Dash of ground cloves
       Nut Sauce
          (recipe follows)
   ⅓ cup pomegranate seeds

Peel fresh chiles, if used, according to instructions on page 14; remove seeds and pithy portions. Cook in boiling salted water about 5 minutes or until tender; drain and cool.

If canned chiles are used, just rinse out seeds and remove any pith. Do not cook.

Sauté onions in the shortening until transparent. Add pork, tomatoes, apples, pears, bananas, nuts, garlic, salt, and cloves. Mix together.

At this point you may stuff the chiles with this mixture (some people like it uncooked), or you may cook it. To cook, stir 15 minutes over medium-high heat, or until any free liquid has evaporated. Cool before using.

Stuff the chiles with either cooked or uncooked mixture and chill.

To serve, arrange several stuffed chiles on individual plates, or place all on one serving platter. Spoon sauce over the top and dot with pomegranate seeds. Serves 6.

Nut Sauce. Put ½ cup milk and ½ cup walnuts in blender container; whirl until nuts are pulverized. Press thick mixture through a wire strainer, discarding nut skins which do not pass through. Put nut-milk mixture back in the blender, add 1 three-oz. package of cream cheese, crumbled, and a dash of salt. Whirl until smooth.

Picadillo Turnovers

EMPANADAS DE PICADILLO
(em-pah-*nah*-thas deh pee-kah-*thee*-yoh)

These turnovers filled with meat, fruit, and nuts are frequently served between meals. You can make them almost any size, to serve as an entrée, a snack, or hor d'oeuvres—miniature ones are called Empanaditas. Empanadas are especially popular at Christmas time.

   ½ pound *each* ground beef and ground pork
          (or 1 lb. ground beef only)
    1 teaspoon butter
    1 large clove garlic, minced or mashed
   ½ cup tomato purée
   ½ cup seedless raisins
   ¼ cup Sherry
    2 teaspoons cinnamon
    1 teaspoon salt
   ½ teaspoon ground cloves
    2 tablespoons vinegar
    1 tablespoon sugar
   ¼ pound (¾ cup) slivered almonds
       Pastry dough made from recipe on page 84
          or pie crust mix (enough for a 9-inch,
          2-crust pie)
       Oil for deep frying (optional)

To prepare what is called *picadillo* filling, brown beef and pork together in butter. Add garlic, tomato purée, raisins, Sherry, cinnamon, salt, cloves, vinegar, and sugar. Cook, uncovered, over medium heat for 20 minutes or until most of the liquid has evaporated. Add almonds; cool.

Prepare pastry dough. Roll out ⅛ inch thick and cut in 3-inch circles for Empanaditas, 4 or 5-inch circles for Empanadas. Spoon filling mixture on one side of each pastry round, moisten edges of pastry, fold over, and seal. Fry in at least 1 inch of oil heated to 370°; or bake in a 400° oven until brown, about 15 to 20 minutes. Makes 3½ dozen Empanaditas or about 15 Empanadas.

Carne Asada Barbecue

CARNE ASADA (kar-neh ah-*sah*-thah)

Carne asada in Spanish means "roasted or barbecued meat," but in some parts of Mexico it is also the name given to a particular dish. There are nearly as many versions of this dish as there are cooks, but one common characteristic is the way the meat is sliced. Beef or pork, usually the tenderloin, is cut in thin strips at a sharp diagonal to the grain of the meat.

The meat is cooked quickly over very hot coals, at the table if you like. Use a Mexican clay *brasero* (see instructions on page 17), Japanese *hibachi*, or other small barbecue. You need a solid bed of well-ignited coals (8 to 16 briquets) 1 to 2 inches below the grill.

Carne Asada Dinner menu includes this dish (see page 17).

     6 mild chorizo sausages (2 to 3 oz. *each*)
       Water
1½ to 1¾ pounds beef tenderloin,
       fat trimmed off
     1 pork tenderloin (about ¾ lb.),
       fat trimmed off
       Coarse (kosher) salt or regular salt
       Sautéed Green Peppers (recipe follows)
       Fried Bananas (recipe follows)

Cover chorizos with cold water, bring to a boil and simmer, covered, for 20 minutes. Drain and let cool.

Cut the beef and pork into diagonal slices about ¼ inch thick and arrange separately on a large tray along with the chorizos. Cook the strips of meat and sausages on a grill 1 or 2 inches above a solid bed of very hot coals. Cook the pork until it loses most of the pink color, then turn to cook evenly until all the pinkness is gone. Cook the beef as you like it. Cook the sausages just until lightly browned and heated through.

Sprinkle coarse salt onto beef and pork before eating. Makes 6 servings.

Sautéed Green Peppers. Wash, seed, and sliver 3 green bell peppers. Melt 1 tablespoon butter in a wide frying pan; add peppers and cook over highest heat, stirring frequently, for about 5 minutes or until peppers are bright green and just beginning to lose their crispness. Keep warm, uncovered, on an electric tray or over a candle warmer.

Fried Bananas. Allow ½ to 1 firm, slightly green-tipped banana for each serving and ½ tablespoon butter for each whole banana. Melt butter in a wide frying pan over medium-low heat. Peel bananas and cut in half lengthwise. Put bananas cut side down in the butter without crowding, and cook over medium-low heat for about 10 minutes or until lightly browned. Carefully turn bananas and cook another 5 to 7 minutes or until lightly browned. Keep warm, uncovered.

Señor Pico Omelet

TORTILLA DE HUEVOS (tor-*tee*-yah theh *weh*-vohs)

The proprietor of several large California Mexican restaurants conceived the idea for this omelet when he saw a Mexican girl sell freshly-cut slivers of green cactus meat at a produce market. Customers would buy a handful, then order scrambled eggs at a nearby restaurant and sprinkle the crisp cactus on top.

More easily obtainable canned or bottled diced cactus (*nopales* or *nopalitos*) gives almost the same crunchiness and flavor to the omelet which resulted from that discovery.

     1 tablespoon butter
       An inch-long slice chorizo sausage,
         skinned and crumbled
     ½ teaspoon minced onion
     3 eggs
     ⅛ teaspoon *each* freshly ground pepper
         and salt
     ½ teaspoon monosodium glutamate
     ¼ canned *jalapeño* chile (seeded) *or*
       ⅛ teaspoon bottled green salsa jalapeña
     2 tablespoons drained diced canned cactus
     1 tablespoon crumbled corn tortilla chips
         (purchased in bags or made by
         instructions on page 30)
     1 tablespoon croutons, sautéed in butter
         (optional)

In an omelet pan (about 8 inches) melt butter, then sauté chorizo and onion until lightly browned. Beat eggs; add pepper, salt, monosodium glutamate, jalapeño chile, cactus, tortilla chips, and croutons if you use them. Pour eggs over onion-sausage mixture and cook over medium-high heat, lifting cooked portion and tilting pan until eggs are almost set. Fold omelet and serve on a warm plate. Makes 1 serving.

Eggs with Avocado Sauce

HUEVOS CON SALSA DE AGUACATES

(*sahl*-sah theh ah-*gooa*-*kah*-tehs)

A good choice for a special-occasion breakfast, these eggs could be accompanied by slices of fried ham or chorizo sausage.

    2 tablespoons minced onion
    2 tablespoons butter
    1 canned California green chile, seeded
        and minced
    1 tablespoon flour
    ½ cup milk
    8 hot hard-cooked eggs
    2 avocados, peeled and seeded
      Salt to taste

Cook onion in butter until limp; add chile, flour, and milk. Cook until thick (this can be done ahead of time). Peel eggs; keep them warm in hot water while you complete the sauce.

Press the avocados through a wire strainer, or whirl smooth in a blender. Stir into the hot milk sauce, season with salt to taste, and pour over the hot drained eggs. Makes 4 servings.

Macaroni & Sausage "Dry Soup"

MACARRÓN CON CHORIZO

(mah-kah-*rrron* kohn choh-*ree*-soh)

The spices in the chorizo sausage are the main flavoring in this hearty Sopa Seca or "dry soup." Most dry soups are simmered on top of the stove, but some like this one are baked in the oven.

    1 pound large tube-shaped macaroni
      Boiling salted water
    1 pound chorizo sausage (purchased or
        made from recipe on page 23)
    2 tablespoons lard or shortening
    ½ cup minced onion
    3 cans (8 oz. each) tomato sauce
    2 tablespoons chopped *cilantro* (Chinese
        parsley or fresh coriander), *or*
      1 teaspoon crumbled oregano
      Salt and pepper
    6 ounces jack cheese, shredded

Boil macaroni in salted water to cover generously until just tender; drain.

Skin chorizo and sauté in the lard until browned. Remove and break meat into pieces.

Cook onion until soft in fat remaining in pan. Add tomato sauce, cilantro or oregano, salt, and pepper. Arrange in a greased 2-quart baking dish in layers: macaroni, chorizo, sauce, and topped with cheese. Bake in a 350° oven for 30 minutes. Serves 6.

Beefsteak, Jalisco Style

BISTEC DE JALISCO (*bees*-tec deh hah-*lees*-koh)

The juice of a fresh orange, mingled with the juices of this barbecued steak, enhances the flavor of the meat rather than adding a detectable fruit accent. The state of Jalisco, in western central Mexico, is the source of this recipe.

Note: Have your meatman make the first cut of beef top round about 2 inches thick (this is the part next to the sirloin); this should make about 3 pounds or more.

Steak Jalisco Barbecue menu includes this dish (see page 19).

    About 3 pounds beef top round
    Salt
    1 orange

Trim off all fat and gash the surface of the steak in a diagonal pattern, making ³/₈-inch-deep cuts about 1 inch apart. Rub the meat lightly with salt. Grill about 5 to 6 inches over medium-hot coals for about 10 minutes on a side for rare meat; or cook to degree of doneness you prefer.

Transfer meat to carving board and squeeze the juice of the orange over the meat. Slice meat vertically and make sure some juice moistens each piece. Makes 8 to 10 servings.

"DRY SOUP" is the Mexican name for pilaf-type dishes like this one of rice, sausage, avocado, and egg.

Green Mole
MOLE VERDE (moh-leh ver-deh)

Mole Verde, a dish of meat with "green *mole*" sauce, gets its characteristic flavor and green color from the *tomatillo*, a walnut-sized sweet green tomato sold fresh or in cans. The more available canned kind are used in the sauce.

    3 to 4 cups sliced cooked turkey, chicken,
        or pork
    2½ cups Green Tomatillo Sauce
        (recipe on page 22)
        Salt
        Small lettuce leaves
        Mild pickled chiles (optional)
        About 1 cup (½ pint) sour cream

Arrange the meat (cut thinly or thickly, as you like) in a wide frying pan and pour the sauce over all. Cover and warm gently over low heat; when the mixture begins to bubble slightly, simmer 5 to 10 minutes. Add salt to taste.

Arrange meat with sauce on a platter. Garnish with lettuce leaves and pickled chiles; serve with sour cream. Serves 4 to 6.

Rice & Sausage "Dry Soup"
SOPA DE ARROZ CON CHORIZO
(soh-pah theh ah-rrros kohn choh-ree-soh)

Avocado and egg slices garnish this colorful Sopa Seca or "dry soup," which is substantial enough to serve as a main dish. (Photo at left.)

    1 pound chorizo sausage (purchased or made
        from recipe on page 23)
    ¼ cup lard or shortening
    2 cups uncooked rice
    ¼ cup minced onion
    ⅓ cup tomato purée
    2 cups fresh peas
    4 cups regular-strength beef or chicken
        broth (or more)
        Salt to taste
    2 hard-cooked eggs
    1 large avocado

Skin chorizo and brown in lard. Mash with a fork; remove and reserve. Brown rice and onion in the same fat. Add chorizo, tomato purée, peas, and stock; cover.

Cook on top of range over medium heat for 25 minutes or in a 350° oven for about 50 minutes, until rice is fluffy. Add more stock if needed; add salt to taste. Just before serving, garnish with slices of egg and avocado. Serves 4 to 6.

Mexican Omelet
TORTILLA DE HUEVOS (tor-tee-yah theh weh-vohs)

A *tortilla* is not only flat, round bread. It also can be an omelet, sometimes called a Tortilla de Huevo to distinguish it from the first kind. Serve with Refried Beans and bread tortillas.

    2 eggs
    1 tablespoon *each* chopped green olives and
        chopped canned California green chiles
    ¼ teaspoon salt
    2 teaspoons butter

Slightly beat eggs. Add chopped olives, chiles, and the salt. Heat butter in a 6 or 7-inch omelet pan. When butter just begins to brown, pour in egg mixture all at once. As soon as the bottom begins to set, lift edges to let the uncooked portion flow into contact with the center of the pan. Turn omelet out of pan. Makes 1 serving.

Turkey Mole

MOLE DE GUAJOLOTE

(*moh*-leh theh gua-hoh-*loh*-teh)

The nuns of a convent in Puebla are supposed to have created this dish more than two centuries ago in honor of a visiting church dignitary. They put practically everything in their kitchen into the creation, which has been a national feast dish ever since. This simplified version uses chile powder instead of many varieties of chile peppers.

Winter Buffet menu includes this dish (see page 18).

12   pound turkey, disjointed (or 4 pounds turkey breasts and 3 pounds turkey thighs)
½   cup flour
1   teaspoon salt
½   cup melted turkey fat, lard, or shortening
    Water
2   teaspoons salt
2   large onions, chopped
1   large clove garlic, chopped
½   cup seedless raisins
2   squares (2 oz.) unsweetened chocolate, cut in small pieces
¼   teaspoon *each* ground anise, coriander, cumin, and cloves
½   cup peanut butter
1   can (8 oz.) tomato sauce
    About ¾ cup chile powder
2   toasted bread slices
3   or 4 corn tortillas, toasted until dry
2   tablespoons sesame seed, toasted
6   cups broth from cooked turkey
1   tablespoon sugar
3   cups raw rice, cooked according to package directions

Rub turkey with flour mixed with 1 teaspoon salt. Brown in turkey fat, lard, or shortening (the Mexicans usually use lard). Put in a large pot, cover with water, add 2 teaspoons salt, and simmer until tender.

Cool, remove bones, and cut meat into large serving pieces. Return bones to stock, adding neck, gizzard, wing tips, and other portions not used. Simmer to make a richly flavored turkey broth.

For *mole* sauce, add onions to pan in which you browned the turkey, and cook until lightly browned, adding more fat if necessary. Add garlic, raisins, chocolate, anise, coriander, cumin, cloves, peanut butter, tomato sauce, and chile powder. Break bread and tortillas into pieces, add with sesame seeds to the onion mixture, and whirl all in a blender until smooth, using 2 cups of turkey broth for the necessary liquid.

(If you don't have a blender, grind the raisins, chocolate, bread, and tortillas through fine blade of a food chopper; mix with the other ingredients; and force through a sieve or food mill.)

Add another 4 cups turkey broth and the sugar. Strain and add more salt or chile powder to taste. Add turkey meat to the mole sauce, heat on top of the range or in the oven, and serve with hot rice. Serves 10 or 12.

Chicken with Rice

ARROZ CON POLLO (ah-*rrros* kohn *poh*-yoh)

Chicken with Rice is colorful with tomatoes and a garnish of peas and asparagus tips. After the initial browning of the meats, all the ingredients cook together in chicken stock until the rice has absorbed the liquid.

Dinner for Guests menu includes this dish (see page 16).

½   pound diced salt pork
3   to 4-pound broiler-fryer chicken, cut in pieces
¼   cup olive oil
½   cup chopped onion
2   tablespoons butter
1   clove garlic, crushed
2   peeled tomatoes or 1 cup drained canned tomatoes, cut in chunks
2   cups uncooked rice
4   cups regular-strength chicken broth or water
2   teaspoons salt
½   teaspoon pepper
    Hot cooked asparagus tips and peas for garnish

Brown pork and set aside. Add chicken and olive oil to pan and brown. Cook onion in butter and add to chicken along with garlic, pork, tomatoes, rice, and broth or water. Add salt and pepper.

Cook, covered, until chicken is tender and rice has absorbed the stock, adding more liquid if necessary to finish cooking the chicken. Serve garnished with asparagus tips and peas. Serves 6 to 8.

Chicken with Oranges

POLLO CON NARANJAS (nah-*rahn*-has)

Imagine yourself on a bougainvillea-covered veranda watching wild parrots flying among mango, papaya, banana, and orange trees. From just such a tropical scene comes this colorful chicken dish, discovered in a restaurant beside the Naranjo ("orange tree") River in east-central Mexico.

4	pound broiler-fryer chicken, cut in pieces
	Salt and pepper
⅛	teaspoon *each* cinnamon and ground cloves
3	tablespoons salad oil
2	cloves garlic
1	medium-sized onion, chopped
1	cup orange juice
1	cup water
	Pinch saffron
2	tablespoons seedless raisins
1	tablespoon capers (or nasturtium seeds)
½	cup coarsely chopped almonds
3	Valencia oranges, peeled and sliced

Sprinkle chicken with salt, pepper, cinnamon, and cloves; brown over moderately high heat in the oil. Add the whole garlic and chopped onion and continue cooking until meat is well browned but not crusted. Add the orange juice, water, saffron, raisins, and capers.

Cover and cook slowly until chicken is tender, about 40 minutes. Add almonds 5 minutes before serving. Remove garlic. Decorate with orange slices. Serves 4 to 6.

Paella

(pah-*ey*-yah)

Paella, the seafood classic, is one of Spain's contributions to the cuisine of Mexico. This dish includes rice and usually both meat and seafood, but beyond that it would be impossible to make a hard-and-fast rule as to what else might be found in it. Paella varies from region to region of Mexico and even from one family to another.

An authentic Paella pan is large, round or oval, and shallow, with a small handle on each side. A large heavy pan, such as a Dutch oven, works satisfactorily.

⅓	cup olive oil, or 2½ tablespoons *each* olive oil and butter
1	pound lean pork spareribs, cut apart
¾	pound chorizo sausages
2	cloves garlic, minced or mashed
3	large tomatoes, peeled and cut into wedges
6	cups water
2	teaspoons salt
¼	teaspoon pepper
1 to 2	dozen small clams in shells (or use mussels when in season)
1 to 1½	pounds shellfish (prawns, shrimp, langostinos, lobster tails, or crayfish)
2	cups uncooked rice
1	can (4 oz.) pimientos, sliced
1	cup fresh or frozen peas
¼	cup chopped parsley

Heat the olive oil in a large heavy pan; add the spareribs and brown well on all sides. Remove casings from chorizos; add to pan and brown. Add garlic, tomatoes, water, salt, pepper. Simmer 20 minutes.

Meanwhile scrub clams or mussels well to remove all sand and barnacles. Shell and remove sand veins from prawns or shrimp; thaw the langostinos or lobster tails, if frozen, and cut lobster tails into 1-inch sections; or drop crayfish into boiling water for about 5 minutes.

Slowly add rice to simmering mixture, then add clams and shellfish. Cook slowly about 20 minutes, stirring occasionally. Add pimientos, peas, and parsley, and cook about 10 minutes longer, or until the rice is tender. Serve immediately to 6 or 8.

Baked Swordfish Manzanillo

PESCADO ESPADA AL HORNO A LA MANZANILLO
(pes-*kah*-thoh es-*pah*-thah ahl *or*-noh man-sah-*nee*-yoh)

Firm-textured, almost meat-flavored swordfish is baked with a generous coating of olive oil and sliced green onions by cooks in the town of Manzanillo on the western coast in the state of Colima.

    4 swordfish steaks (about 8 oz. *each*)
 1½ teaspoons salt
   ⅛ teaspoon pepper
    6 tablespoons olive oil
   ½ cup sliced green onions
       Chopped parsley
       Tomato and lime wedges

Sprinkle swordfish steaks with salt and pepper. Place fish in a single layer in a baking dish; brush with olive oil to coat heavily. Sprinkle green onions over the fish.

Bake uncovered in a 350° oven for about 20 minutes, or until fish flakes easily with a fork. Remove to platter and serve sprinkled with parsley and garnished with tomato and lime wedges. Makes 4 servings.

Fried Almond Shrimp

CAMARÓN FRITO (kah-mah-*ron free*-toh)

In a garden restaurant overlooking Bocochibampo Bay near Guaymas in northern Mexico, you can have your own freshly caught fish cooked, or you may be able to get a portion of another's catch from the kitchen. Failing that, you may order this delectable dish of shrimp from the bay.

    1 pound extra-large shrimps (26-30 per lb.)
    1 egg
   ½ cup milk
   ¾ cup flour
   ¼ teaspoon crumbled oregano
   ¼ teaspoon garlic salt
   ⅛ teaspoon pepper
       About ¼ cup coarsely chopped
          blanched almonds
       Salad oil or shortening for deep frying

Remove shells from shrimps, but leave the last section of shell and the tail. Slice each shrimp along vein deeply enough to lay out flat, butterfly fashion; remove and discard vein.

Beat together until smooth the egg, milk, flour, and seasonings. Dip shrimps in batter, allow to drain a moment, and spread in a single layer on a tray. Sprinkle with almonds. Chill 2 hours.

Note: To coat shrimp with more almonds, dip batter-coated shrimp into the nuts rather than sprinkling them on.

Drop into deep fat heated to 370°; cook until golden brown. Drain on absorbent paper. Serve hot. Makes 3 or 4 servings.

Breaded Fish

PESCADO EMPANADO (em-pah-*nah*-thoh)

Perched on a rocky shoreline cliff on the southern tip of Baja California is a hotel whose dining room specializes in sauces made from recipes collected throughout Mexico. One such sauce is the following marinade for the fish or shellfish which are to be dipped in crumbs and sautéed.

   ⅓ cup lemon juice
    2 tablespoons dry white wine
   ¼ cup *each* salad oil and minced onion
    1 or 2 small cloves garlic, minced or mashed
 1½ teaspoons crumbled oregano
    1 teaspoon salt
   ¼ teaspoon pepper
    1 to 3 pounds scallops, large shelled shrimp,
          oysters, or fish fillets
       Egg coating (1 tablespoon milk beaten
          with each egg used)
       Fine dry bread crumbs
       Salad oil (or part oil and part butter)
       Tartar sauce (optional)

To make marinade, combine lemon juice, wine, oil, onion, garlic, oregano, salt, and pepper. Place fish in marinade, turning pieces to coat all sides. Let stand about 20 minutes.

Lift fish from marinade; drain well. (Save marinade to re-use if desired; it will keep several days in the refrigerator.) Dip fish in egg coating, then coat with bread crumbs. Place pieces, not touching each other, in single layer on waxed paper; let stand 5 minutes.

Brown fish on all sides in a small amount of hot oil (or oil and butter combined). Serve with tartar sauce if desired. Makes 3 to 9 servings, depending upon the amount of fish prepared.

APPETIZERS & TIDBITS

For important meals or those parties called "el coctel"

Mexicans are so accustomed to snacking whenever hungry that it is no wonder a variety of tidbits suitable for appetizers are typical of the cuisine.

In fact, some of the foods served by restaurants in the United States as main dishes are eaten mainly as snacks or appetizers in Mexico. The well-known Tacos are a prime example. Tacos are sold by street vendors for between-meal eating. They may even be prepared over a charcoal brazier at the most posh cocktail party by someone hired for the task, perhaps a handsome Indian woman wearing regional costume.

Tacos and all the other appetite-creating or appetite-sating foods are called *antojos* ("whims") or *antojitos* ("little whims"), depending on their size.

To turn these "whims" into party appetizers, the cook may simply serve them in smaller quantity or greater variety. Or she may make them in a smaller size. Tamales prepared in miniature are called Tamalitos, or "little tamales." The meat-filled turnovers, Empanadas, are likewise called by the diminutive, Empanaditas, when made diminutive size.

The word antojitos also is the term used to describe a particular kind of "whim" made with a masa (corn tortilla flour) dough similar to that used for Tamales. The dough is shaped into small circles, boat shapes, or rimmed discs and then deep-fried. A variety of meat, bean, cheese, and vegetable toppings may be added. The four most familiar kinds are called Gorditas, Sopes, Garnaches, and Chalupas. All of these except Garnaches are small enough for appetizers made ordinary size. And Garnaches are easily prepared half-size if necessary.

Recipes for the various antojos and antojitos are not included in the following chapter because you will usually serve them as main dishes. But don't forget that they can be appetizers, particularly if you plan a guest meal of dishes which are authentic but not what some people think of as Mexican.

Recipes for the double-duty "whims" will be found on the pages indicated: Tacos (several kinds), page 30; Quesadillas, 32; Tostadas, 33 and 34; Tamales, 47; Gorditas, 49; Sopes, 50; Garnaches, 50; Chalupas, 51; and Picadillo Turnovers (Empanadas), 57.

Many of the appetizer recipes on the succeeding pages feature seafood, a much more popular and available food than those only acquainted with American Mexican restaurants may realize. Several of the best-loved first-course dishes feature fish rather than the shellfish often served at the beginning of full-course meals in the United States. Marinated Fish (Escabeche), in the salad chapter on page 74, is also served as an appetizer.

If you don't want to prepare special appetizers and prefer something simple like potato chips or nuts with drinks before dinner, consider Pepitas, toasted and salted pumpkin seeds. These are sold in jars at many supermarkets and gourmet shops. Pepitas are omnipresent at Mexican parties.

Guacamole

Guacamole, always popular as an appetizer, is more than that in Mexico. It is an all-purpose avocado sauce which may appear with many dishes. For this reason, the recipe (with several variations) is included with the basic sauces and fillings chapter on page 21.

You may serve Guacamole as an appetizer with corn chips you buy, but the most tasty dippers are freshly fried corn tortilla chips, also called Tostadas. Instructions for frying them are on page 30.

Refried Bean Dip

APERITIVO DE FRIJOLES REFRITOS
(ah-pe-ree-*tee*-voh theh free-*hoh*-less rrreh-*free*-tohs)

This refried bean dip with cheese is heated, then kept hot over slow coals or candle warmer.

    1 can (1 lb.) Refried Beans
    1 cup (¼ lb.) shredded Cheddar cheese
    ½ cup chopped green onion, including
          part of the tops
    ¼ teaspoon salt
    2 to 3 tablespoons Taco sauce
       Crisp-fried corn tortilla chips (also called
       Tostadas)—see instructions on page 30
       or use packaged tortilla or corn chips

Mix together the Refried Beans, cheese, green onion, salt, and Taco sauce. Place in a small pan or heatproof Mexican pottery bowl. Cook over low heat or slow coals in a barbecue, stirring, until heated. Keep warm; serve with tortilla chips for "dippers." Makes about 3 cups.

Oaxacan Peanuts

CACAHUETES (kah-kah-*ooeh*-tehs)

These nuts improve with standing, especially if stirred occasionally. In Mexico they use whole peeled garlic and leave it with the peanuts, but the danger of losing a friend who eats a clove of it instead of a peanut has prompted the method described.

    20 small, dried red chiles (*serrano* chiles or
           others about 1 inch long)
     4 cloves garlic, finely minced or pressed
     2 tablespoons olive oil
     2 pounds blanched, salted Virginia peanuts
     1 teaspoon coarse salt (use a salt mill or
           kosher salt)
     1 teaspoon chile powder

Heat chiles, garlic, and olive oil in a heavy pan for 1 minute. Stir so the chiles won't scorch.

Mix in the peanuts and stir over medium heat, or spread on a cooky sheet and bake in a 350° oven for 5 minutes, or until slightly brown.

Sprinkle with coarse salt and chile powder. Mix well and store in a covered jar or tin at least a day before serving.

Shellfish Cocktail with Lime

MARISCOS CON LIMÓN
(mah-*rees*-kohs kohn lee-*mohn*)

Seafood is a specialty of eating places near the beautiful Bahía de la Concepción at Mulegé where you can gather some delicious things to eat from the beach almost as easily as you can pick up pebbles.

At some spots you can sift Pismo and butter clams from the sand with your fingers. At the mouth of the bay, you can dive in shallow water to pry free meaty rock scallops, which are used by a local chef in this refreshing cocktail. Shrimp also take well to the cocktail sauce flavored with lime juice and lime peel.

    1½ pounds raw scallops or deveined, shelled,
           and cooked shrimp (30 or
           40-to-the-pound size)
     ¼ teaspoon grated lime peel
     ¼ cup lime juice
     ¼ cup dry white wine
     ½ cup catsup
     3 or 4 drops liquid hot-pepper seasoning
        Salt and pepper to taste

If scallops are used, first poach them in 1½ cups simmering salted water or white wine, just until they lose their translucence throughout, about 8 to 10 minutes.

Place scallops or shrimp in a deep bowl. Mix together lime peel and juice, wine, catsup, and liquid hot-pepper seasoning; pour over seafood. Mix well and season with salt and pepper. Cover and chill well. Makes 6 servings.

Cheese-Tortilla Appetizers
TOSTADAS DE HARINA
(tohs-tah-thas deh ah-ree-nah)

Flour tortillas make a crisp, tasty base for these hot appetizers. You can also serve them as accompaniments for soup or salad.

Midnight Christmas Eve Supper menu includes this dish (see page 19).

6 flour tortillas (7 inches in diameter)
2 cups shredded mild Cheddar cheese
2 tablespoons seeded and chopped canned
    California green chiles *or* 2 chorizo
    sausages *or* ½ can (12-oz. size) corned beef

Note: To prepare chorizo or corned beef, crumble meat and cook until lightly browned; drain off excess fat.

Evenly sprinkle tortillas with shredded cheese, leaving about a ½-inch margin around edges. Top with chopped green chiles, cooked chorizo, or corned beef. Bake on ungreased baking sheets in a 425° oven for 8 to 10 minutes or until edges are crisp and browned. Cut each tortilla into 6 wedges; serve hot. Makes 3 dozen.

Grilled Cheese
QUESO AL HORNO (*keh*-soh ahl *or*-noh)

Grill this cheese over very slow coals in a brazier, perhaps a Mexican *brasero* or Japanese *hibachi*. If your fire is too hot, the cheese will burn on the bottom and boil over. When cheese has completely melted, remove from fire; return to heat occasionally to keep warm and melted as it is served.

Instructions for firing the fragile clay braseros are included with the Carne Asada menu on page 17).

1 to 1¼ pounds jack cheese
    Fresh Tomato and Green Chile Sauce
    (recipe on page 20)
12 corn tortillas

Slice cheese in ¼-inch-thick slices; place a single layer in an 8-inch pottery or heatproof dish, or a cake or pie pan ½ to ¾ inch deep. Cover and set aside.

Make fresh chile sauce. One-half the quantity

produced by the basic recipe (1½ cups) will be enough for these appetizers.

Heat tortillas by placing them, one at a time, on a medium-hot griddle or in an ungreased heavy frying pan over medium-high heat; heat about 30 seconds on a side, or just until soft. Stack tortillas and cut in quarters. Wrap in a tea towel or foil and keep in a warm place until you are ready to serve.

Place plate of cheese to melt over *very slow* charcoal. Have your guests make their own appetizers by spreading some of the softened cheese on a tortilla wedge, spooning on a little of the chile sauce, then folding tortilla wedge to enclose the filling. Makes about 48 appetizers.

Fish Appetizer, Acapulco Style
SEVICHE DE ACAPULCO (seh-*vee*-cheh)

Seviche, a popular appetizer in Mexico, is made from raw fish or shellfish cooked without heat by marinating in lime or lemon juice. The seafood looks and tastes as though it has been poached. It is white and firm and has lost any raw, translucent look.

Dinner for Guests menu includes this dish (see page 16).

1½ pounds mild-flavored fish fillets *or*
    raw scallops
  1 cup lemon or lime juice (about 5 lemons or
    6 limes)
  2 canned California green chiles,
    seeded and chopped
½ cup minced onion
  2 large tomatoes, peeled, seeded, and
    cut in pieces
  1 teaspoon salt
¼ teaspoon crumbled oregano
¼ cup olive oil
    Avocado slices, canned California green
    chile strips, pimiento strips, or chopped
    cilantro (fresh coriander or Chinese
    parsley) for garnish

Cut fish in small, thin pieces; if scallops are used, dice or thinly slice them. Cover raw seafood with lemon or lime juice and let stand covered, in the refrigerator, 2 hours. Then mix with all remaining ingredients.

Serve very cold in cocktail or sherbet glasses, decorated with one or two of the suggested garnishes. Serves 8 to 12 as appetizer.

Jícama Appetizer

JÍCAMA FRESCA (hee-kah-mah fres-kah)

Jícama, a crisp root vegetable, is sold by street vendors in Mexico in this fashion to eat as refreshment. For a complete description of jícama and where you may buy it in this country, see page 10. (Photo at right.)

    1 tablespoon salt
    ¼ teaspoon chile powder
    1 to 2 pounds jícama, peeled
    1 lime, cut in wedges

Blend salt with chile powder and put in a small bowl. Slice the jícama in ¼ to ½-inch-thick slices and arrange on a serving tray with the bowl of the seasoned salt and lime wedges.

To eat, rub lime over jícama, then dip in the salt. Serves 6 to 8.

Butterflied Shrimp

APERITIVO DE CAMARÓN
(ah-pe-ree-tee-voh theh kah-mah-ron)

Barbecue these skewered appetizers over hot coals, basting occasionally with lime or lemon juice in melted butter. Squeeze more lime juice over the shrimp at the last minute before serving.

    1 pound raw jumbo to medium-sized shrimp
    1 egg, slightly beaten
    ¼ teaspoon each salt and pepper
      About ½ cup fine dry bread crumbs
    ½ cup melted butter
    ¼ cup lime or lemon juice
      Lime wedges

Remove shells, tails, and veins from the shrimp. Slit shrimp down the back side, cutting almost all the way through so you can lay it out flat (take care not to cut entirely in half).

Dip shrimp in egg slightly beaten with the salt and pepper, then in the bread crumbs to coat each side. Thread each shrimp on a single, long, thin bamboo skewer. Insert point of skewer at tail of shrimp and impale its full length so that the point of skewer just shows at head end of shrimp. Refrigerate until ready to cook.

Cook over hot coals; baste occasionally with a mixture of the butter and lime or lemon juice. Serve with lime wedges. Makes 16 to 25.

RAW JÍCAMA slices, crisp and white, are appetizing rubbed with lime and dipped in chile powder-salt mixture.

Skewered Swordfish & Cantaloupe

PESCADO ESPADA Y MELÓN A LA BROCHETA
(es-pah-thah ee meh-lohn ah lah bro-cheh-tah)

Skewered cubes of fish and cantaloupe, a strange but compatible combination, cook so quickly over charcoal that guests may do their own.

    1 pound swordfish
    ¾ cup lime or lemon juice
    2 tablespoons chopped green onion
    ¼ teaspoon salt
    1 large cantaloupe
      Lime wedges

Cut swordfish into ¾-inch cubes. Place in a large bowl and cover with a marinade of the lime or lemon juice, chopped green onion, and salt. Cover and chill in marinade 1 hour. Remove rind and seeds from the cantaloupe; cut in ½-inch cubes.

Alternate cubes of swordfish and cantaloupe on long thin wooden skewers; allow three cubes per appetizer. Cook over hot coals. Serve with lime wedges. Makes about 25 appetizers.

LIGHT & HEARTY SOUPS

Broths to whet the appetite or robust brews to make a meal

Soup is an important part of the *comida*, the big meal of the day. The soup which begins a comida usually is a light one. But Mexican brews run the gamut from clear broths to rib-sticking concoctions of several meats and vegetables to which fresh vegetable relishes may also be added at serving time. Cream soups of a light nature are often served, too.

Right after the soup at the comida, another dish called a Sopa Seca or "dry soup" may be served if the meal is a fiesta or formal occasion.

No one is certain how this name originated, for dry soups are not soups at all. They are rice, pasta, hominy, or other starchy dishes comparable to the pasta or pilaf courses in the cookery of other countries. The quantity of liquid required in their preparation may have some bearing on the name. They probably are of Spanish origin. Natives may have applied the dry-soup term for want of a better name, or even as a small joke.

Nevertheless, dry soups are not soups and would not be served as such in an American-style meal. Therefore, the recipes for them are included in the chapter on rice, beans, and other starchy accompaniments (page 79) *if* they are suitable for accompanying a main dish.

One of these is the rice which accompanies most blue-plate specials in American Mexican restaurants. Being a dry soup, this rice would be served *before* the entrée in Mexico.

Some dry soups containing meat, seafood, or eggs are hearty enough to be a main dish. The recipes for these are printed in the Main Dish Specialties chapter (pages 59 and 60); they are casserole-type dishes convenient for making ahead.

The soups on the following pages are all "wet" and soupy in the way you would expect. Several of them are filling enough to be main dishes if served in sufficiently large portions and accompanied by plenty of soft, hot tortillas or crisp-fried tortilla chips.

You will find two recipes here for Gazpacho, a cold soup containing raw chopped vegetables, which can double as a salad. Although made similarly, these two Gazpachos are quite different in ingredients and flavor.

Sonorese Corn Soup

SOPA SONORENSE (soh-pah soh-noh-ren-seh)

Named for the state of Sonora, this soup is based on chicken broth plus a mingling of the sweet, mild flavors of green pepper, corn, and chile powder. Whipped cream piled into the hot soup just before serving dissolves deliciously into each portion.

2 tablespoons butter
1 teaspoon chile powder
2 cups largely diced green bell pepper
1 can (12 oz.) whole kernel corn with red and green sweet peppers
1 small, dry, whole hot red pepper
6 cups regular-strength chicken broth
    Salt to taste
1 cup whipping cream
¼ teaspoon salt

Melt butter in a saucepan and stir in chile powder and green pepper. Cook, stirring, over moderate heat for about 3 minutes. Then add corn, red pepper, and broth and bring to a boil, uncovered. Let simmer about 3 minutes; salt to taste, if needed.

Whip cream with ¼ teaspoon salt until stiff. Pour soup into tureen and pile the whipped cream on top. Stir slightly and ladle mixture from bottom of dish (the corn settles) into individual bowls. Makes 8 to 10 servings.

Tomato Gazpacho with Avocado

(gahs-*pah*-cho)

To keep Gazpacho cold, add several ice cubes to each serving bowl.

½ cucumber, peeled if you like
½ mild red or white onion, peeled
½ avocado, peeled
½ teaspoon crumbled oregano
3 tablespoons olive oil or salad oil
2 tablespoons wine vinegar
4 cups canned tomato juice
  Ice cubes
2 limes, cut in wedges

Cut off a few slices of cucumber and onion; save for garnish. Chop rest of cucumber and onion in small pieces; slice or chop avocado. Put onion, cucumber, avocado, oregano, oil, and vinegar in a serving bowl. Pour in the tomato juice. Top with cucumber and onion slices; chill.

Ladle into bowls, adding 2 or 3 ice cubes and lime juice to taste. Serves 6.

Asparagus with Cream Cheese

CALDO DE ESPÁRRAGO CON QUESO
(*kah*l-doh thes-*pah*-rrrah-goh kohn *keh*-soh)

To this typical light soup of asparagus pieces cooked in chicken broth, you have the option of adding melting chunks of cream cheese or spoonfuls of cool, thick sour cream.

1 package (10 oz.) frozen cut asparagus
4 cups regular-strength chicken broth
  Salt
2 small packages (3 oz. *each*) cream cheese
  or 1 cup sour cream

Combine the asparagus and broth in a saucepan and bring to boiling, uncovered. Stir to break apart asparagus and simmer gently, uncovered, for 10 minutes. Add salt to taste, if needed.

Cut the cream cheese into about ½-inch cubes and place in a soup tureen. Pour in the hot asparagus soup and serve at once. Or instead of using the cream cheese, you can pass sour cream to spoon into individual servings of the soup. Makes 6 to 8 servings.

Tripe & Hominy Soup

MENUDO (meh-*noo*-doh)

Menudo is a soup of tripe and corn in some form, usually *nixtamal* made from dried corn. Canned hominy makes a good substitute.

The soup traditionally is served on Christmas or New Year's eves—or any other evening when over-celebration might cause that morning-after feeling. Some Mexican men out on the town stop at all-night cafes for a Menudo nightcap, because a bowlful is said to be good preventive medicine for hangovers.

Midnight Christmas Eve Supper menu includes this dish (see page 19).

5 pounds tripe
1 large veal knuckle
4 cloves garlic
1 tablespoon salt
2 cups chopped onion
1 teaspoon minced *cilantro* (also called fresh coriander or Chinese parsley), optional
1 tablespoon chile powder (or to taste) *or* 1 can (4 oz.) California green chiles, seeded and chopped
1 gallon water
1 large can (1 lb. 13 oz.) whole hominy
2 tablespoons lemon juice
2 cups chopped green onions
1½ cups chopped *cilantro or* fresh mint (or 1 cup dry mint leaves)

Cut tripe in oblong pieces or slivers. Put in a large pot along with the veal, garlic, salt, bulb onion, cilantro, chile powder, and water. Cover and simmer for about 6 hours, or until tripe is tender, adding more water if necessary.

Add hominy and heat; then add lemon juice and serve with chopped green onions and cilantro or mint. Serves 6 to 8.

POZOLE (Pork and Hominy Soup) is enhanced by fresh tidbits added just before eating. Here chopped green onions, diced radishes, avocado cubes, and shredded cheese are offered in side dishes.

Pork & Hominy Soup

POZOLE (poh-*soh*-leh)

This interesting soup has many versions, all containing pork (often a pig's head) and either hominy or corn. The following kind is made from inexpensive pork hocks (the meaty ends cut from front legs of fresh pork).

2 large fresh pork hocks, split in 2 or 3 pieces each
2 quarts water
1 can (1 lb.) whole tomatoes
2 cans (1 lb. *each*) hominy, drained
2 medium-sized onions, finely chopped
4 teaspoons salt
   Fresh vegetable relishes: shredded lettuce,
     chopped radishes, thinly sliced green
     onions, shredded carrots, or chopped
     avocado
   Cubes of cream cheese or other soft cheese
     such as jack, shredded
2 limes, cut in wedges
   Liquid hot-pepper seasoning, chopped
     chiles, or horseradish (optional)

Put the pork hocks into a large kettle with the water, tomatoes, hominy, onions, and salt. Simmer for 2 to 3 hours, or until the meat begins to come away from the bones.

Remove pork hocks from soup; cool both meat and soup. Remove meat from the hocks, discarding fat and bones; cut the meat into small pieces. When the soup is cold, skim off the fat. Just before serving, add meat to soup and heat, adding additional salt if needed.

Serve with an assortment of chopped fresh vegetables, cheese, and lime wedges to be added to individual servings.

You might also provide hot-pepper seasoning, chopped fresh or canned hot chiles, or horseradish for those who prefer hotter seasonings.

Makes 8 to 10 servings.

Note: Photograph above shows Pozole with the assortment of vegetable relishes and cheese in individual bowls. Hot corn sticks (pictured) or warm corn tortillas are excellent accompaniments.

To complete an easily prepared meal suitable for family or guests, add a make-ahead dessert, such as one of the custards in the desserts chapter on page 84.

Clear Gazpacho

(gahs-*pah*-cho)

The cold soup called Gazpacho probably originated with Spanish peasants and has been adopted by Mexico. Many variations are made in both countries with either cold water, meat broth, or tomato juice as the liquid. A variety of chopped raw vegetables, citrus juice or vinegar for piquancy, and olive oil may be added.

The result, of course, is a soupy salad. You may serve Gazpacho as soup, salad, or dual-purpose dish with many types of Mexican meals.

    4 cups regular-strength chicken broth, chilled
    4 medium-sized tomatoes, chopped
    ½ teaspoon seasoned pepper
    2 tablespoons olive oil or salad oil
    6 to 8 tablespoons fresh lime juice
         (about 3 limes)
       Salt to taste
    1 small red onion, finely chopped
    1 or 2 green bell peppers, finely chopped
    1 or 2 stalks celery, finely chopped
       Lime slices and watercress sprigs for
         garnish (optional)

Remove any fat from broth and discard. Mix with tomatoes (including juices), pepper, oil, lime juice (taste for tartness desired), and salt. Chill thoroughly. Serve from a tureen or bowl, ladling into dishes and offering individual containers of onion, green pepper, and celery to add according to personal preference. Garnish bowls with lime and watercress. Makes 4 to 6 servings.

Tomato-Pepper Cream Soup

CALDO LARGO (*kahl*-doh *lar*-goh)

From La Paz on the Baja coast comes this version of Caldo Largo. *Caldo* is the word for broth, but *largo* generally means "long." It's a puzzle how a soup can be long, so one of the other meanings of the word may be intended, perhaps "abundant." All the ingredients for this soup are indeed abundant and usually on hand in the typical kitchen there.

Another explanation for the name might be that the soup was originally made with the largo variety of chile, a long pepper.

Whatever the meaning of the name, the long or short of it is: It's a good soup.

    2 tablespoons salad oil
    2 medium-sized tomatoes, peeled, seeded,
         and diced
    2 medium-sized green bell peppers, seeded
         and cut in thin strips
    1½ cups regular-strength chicken broth
    1 can (14½ oz.) evaporated milk
       Salt
       Liquid hot-pepper seasoning
    ¼ pound jack cheese, diced

Heat oil in a wide pan, add tomatoes and peppers and cook until peppers are limp. Add broth and simmer slowly for about 10 minutes. Stir in milk; add salt and liquid hot-pepper seasoning to taste. Mix in the cheese and ladle immediately into soup bowls. Serves 4 to 6.

Meatball Soup

SOPA DE ALBÓNDIGAS (al-*bohn*-dee-gahs)

This simplified version of Mexican meatball soup has a clear consommé base touched with Sherry. The little meatballs are filled with pine nuts instead of the more usual rice. However, such variations are typical. Cooks like to alter these meatballs by tucking some kind of a "surprise" inside each, such as an olive, or by changing the seasonings.

    1 pound ground beef round
    ¾ teaspoon salt
    ¾ teaspoon chile powder
    1 small onion, grated
    1 cup fine dry bread crumbs
    ½ cup pine nuts
    1 egg, slightly beaten
    2 cans (10½ oz. *each*) condensed consommé
    2 cans water
    1 bay leaf
    ¼ cup dry Sherry

Mix together ground round, salt, chile powder, onion, bread crumbs, pine nuts, and egg. Shape into tiny meatballs about 1 inch in diameter or smaller.

Pour consommé, water, and bay leaf into a saucepan; cover and bring to a boil. Add meatballs, a few at a time so that boiling is constant. Reduce heat, cover, and simmer for 30 minutes.

Just before serving, remove bay leaf and stir in Sherry. Makes 4 to 6 servings.

COLORFUL SALADS

Appealing ways to brighten a meal with fruits and vegetables

Salads are not an important part of the cuisine. A few kinds are prepared, but usually fruits and vegetables are worked into the diet other ways.

The great variety of temperate-zone and tropical fruits are usually eaten fresh and *au naturel*, for dessert or snacks. Citrus fruits and their juices are used in many kinds of dishes.

Vegetable salads, particularly the mixed green type, are rarely seen. But many dishes are garnished with chopped lettuce, onion, radishes, or avocado in some form, often mashed into Guacamole. The cold soup, Gazpacho, contains a variety of raw vegetables. Many hot soups contain cooked vegetables, and a few are garnished with raw, chopped ones at serving time. Both the chile peppers and tomatoes used in innumerable dishes and sauces are laden with several important vitamins.

Salads as such may be few, but the dietary benefits of them are not lacking.

With any Mexican meal crisp raw vegetable relishes, olives, and pickled peppers (presented on a bed of crushed ice if you like) may be all the salad food you need serve. Or you may begin with a bowl of chilled Gazpacho, a soup which has all the light refreshing effect of a salad. Two Gazpacho recipes are on pages 69 and 71.

Whenever the weather or mood calls for a main-dish salad, you may serve one of several popular specialties included in other chapters.

The Topopo (page 35), which really could be called a chef's salad, consists of a crisp tortilla laden with shredded lettuce, a mixed vegetable salad, meat or seafood, and cheese.

The more familiar Tostada has such a quantity of lettuce, Guacamole, and vegetable garnish that it can double as a salad. Several kinds are printed on pages 33 and 34.

Three salads, of meat or fish, in this chapter can serve as main dishes—both Marinated Fish and the Tongue and Vegetable Salad on page 74, and the Marinated Beef Salad on page 75.

Christmas Eve Salad
ENSALADA DE NOCHEBUENA
(en-sah-*la*-thah theh noh-cheh-*booeh*-nah)

After Christmas Eve mass or the midnight hour, a supper which traditionally includes this salad and one of several classic turkey dishes is served.

Midnight Christmas Eve Supper menu includes this dish (see page 19).

8 small cooked beets
4 oranges, peeled (white membrane removed)
4 red apples, unpeeled but cored
4 bananas, peeled
1 fresh pineapple, peeled and cored, or 1 can (1 lb. 14 oz.) pineapple chunks
3 limes, peeled (white membrane removed)
1 head iceberg lettuce
¼ cup sugar (optional)
Seeds of 2 pomegranates
1 cup peanuts, chopped
1 cup tart French dressing (¾ cup oil, ¼ cup red wine vinegar, salt) *or* 1 cup orange juice

Thinly slice the beets, oranges, apples, bananas, pineapple (if fresh), and limes. Shred the lettuce.

Put lettuce in the bottom of a large shallow bowl and arrange fruits over it, sprinkling with the sugar, if you choose to use it. Arrange top layer attractively, perhaps with a ring of oranges around the outer edge, then beets, then pineapple in the center, with pomegranate seeds and chopped peanuts sprinkled over all.

Just before serving, pour on the French dressing or the orange juice; mix gently. Serves 8.

Kidney Bean Salad

ENSALADA DE FRIJOLES (free-*hoh*-less)

There's an interesting texture play in this salad: crisp celery, crunchy nuts, and meaty beans. Although you can prepare it a day in advance, it will be crisper if you assemble it just a few hours ahead.

Summer Buffet menu includes this dish (see page 16).

    1 can (about 1 lb.) red kidney beans
    2 cups chopped celery
    1 tablespoon minced onion
    ½ cup chopped walnuts
    4 small sweet pickles, chopped
    ¼ cup salad oil
    3 tablespoons wine vinegar
    ½ teaspoon *each* salt and pepper
       Lettuce (if desired)

Drain beans thoroughly; combine with celery, onion, nuts, and pickles. Mix the oil, vinegar, salt, and pepper; pour over bean-celery mixture; toss. Serve on lettuce, if you wish. Serves 8.

Jícama Pico de Gallo

PICO DE GALLO CON JÍCAMA
(*pee*-koh theh *gah*-yoh kohn *hee*-kah-mah)

The most typical Pico de Gallo salad contains the sweet, crunchy root vegetable, *jícama*. See page 10 for a complete description and tips about where it may be purchased.

Steak Jalisco Barbecue menu includes this dish (see page 19).

    2 cups peeled and diced raw *jícama*
    1 green bell pepper, seeded and slivered
    ½ medium-sized mild onion, thinly sliced
    1 cup sliced or diced cucumber
    ¼ cup olive oil
    2 tablespoons white or red wine vinegar
    ½ teaspoon crumbled oregano
       Salt
       Pepper

Combine jícama, green pepper, onion, and cucumber. Pour olive oil and vinegar over vegetables and mix lightly with oregano. Add salt and pepper to taste. Makes 4 to 6 servings.

Orange Pico de Gallo

PICO DE GALLO ANARANJADO
(*pee*-koh theh *gah*-yoh a-nar-an-*hah*-tho)

Many versions of Pico de Gallo are made with a variety of ingredients, usually chopped or cut into chunks. The name meaning "rooster's bill" refers to the old-style way of eating the salad by picking up the chunks with the fingers, which resembles the way a rooster pecks corn.

In this version, the cut-up ingredients are served over a bed of romaine, making forks preferable to fingers.

Steak Jalisco Barbecue menu includes this dish (see page 19).

    2 quarts crisp, broken pieces of romaine
    1 medium-sized orange, peeled and thinly
       sliced
    ½ cucumber, thinly sliced
    ½ sweet onion, slivered
    ½ green bell pepper, diced
    ½ to 1 cup raw, peeled, and chopped *jícama*,
       optional (see shopping instructions on
       page 10)
       Small romaine leaves (optional)
    ½ cup salad oil or olive oil
    ⅓ cup wine vinegar
    ½ teaspoon salt

Place romaine in a salad bowl. Arrange on the greens the orange, cucumber, onion, green pepper, and jícama if available. Garnish rim of the salad with tips of inner romaine leaves, if you desire.

Blend oil with wine vinegar and salt. Pour dressing over salad and mix lightly to serve. Makes 8 servings.

Marinated Fish

ESCABECHE (es-kah-*beh*-cheh)

Escabeche, which means "pickled," here consists of cooked fish chilled in a spicy marinade and colorfully garnished. Sometimes tongue, brains, or other meats are used, but fish is the most familiar main ingredient. This dish usually is an appetizer-salad, but could be a main dish.

    2 pounds mild-flavored fish steaks
    ½ cup olive oil
    1 large onion, sliced
    2 cloves garlic, peeled
    2 canned California green chiles,
         seeded and chopped
    ½ cup vinegar
    ¼ teaspoon ground cumin
    1 teaspoon salt
       Juice of 1 orange
       Lettuce, sliced oranges, ripe olives, and
         sliced hard-cooked eggs for garnish

Sauté fish steak in olive oil on both sides until lightly browned. Arrange in a shallow serving dish. In the same pan, cook the onion and the whole garlic cloves (threaded on a toothpick) until lightly browned.

Discard garlic; add green chiles, vinegar, cumin, salt, and the orange juice. Pour over the fish and chill. Serve with the garnishes. Serves 8.

Orange Salad

ENSALADA DE NARANJAS (nah-*rahn*-has)

This version of orange and onion salad has chile powder seasonings.

Summer Buffet menu includes this (page 16).

    5 large oranges
    1 white onion, thinly sliced
    ⅓ cup salad oil
    ¼ cup wine vinegar
    1 teaspoon sugar
    ½ teaspoon salt
    ¼ teaspoon chile powder
       Paprika

Peel oranges, cutting away white membrane, and slice. Arrange orange and onion slices alternately in a bowl. Mix the oil, vinegar, sugar, salt, chile powder; pour over the salad. Sprinkle with paprika. If you wish, serve on crisp lettuce. Serves 8.

Tongue & Vegetable Salad

SALPICÓN (sahl-pee-*kohn*)

Salpicón translates into English as "salmagundi," or—if you need help on that word—a salad-like dish featuring meat with vegetables and dressing. Start this supper salad a day ahead so the cooked meat and vegetables can chill.

Complete the menu with warm, soft corn tortillas and butter, cold Mexican beer or orange juice, and Caramel Custard (recipe on page 89).

   2½ to 3-pound beef tongue
    2 quarts water
    1 *each* carrot, sliced onion, and celery stalk
    ¼ cup white wine vinegar
    1 teaspoon salt
    ½ teaspoon whole black pepper
    1 teaspoon whole oregano
    ¼ teaspoon whole cumin seed
       Tongue Marinade and Cooked Vegetables
         (directions follow)
       Shredded lettuce and a few leaves
       Parsley and sliced sweet onion rings

Scrub tongue well under running water, then place in a large pan. Add water, carrot, onion, celery, vinegar, salt, pepper, oregano, and cumin. Cover and bring to boiling, then reduce heat to simmer and cook 2½ to 3 hours or until meat is quite tender. Let cool in broth.

Remove tongue, reserving liquid, and skin tongue, trimming away any fat and bones. Slice tongue thinly and place in a deep bowl. Pour Tongue Marinade over meat and chill, covered, overnight.

Meantime, pour broth through wire strainer; discard residue. Skim fat from broth (or chill and lift off fat); use this as cooking liquid for the vegetables.

To serve, cover a large platter with shredded lettuce and arrange on top the tongue and cooked vegetables. Pour over all the meat marinade and enough vegetable marinade to moisten Salpicón lightly. Decorate platter with lettuce leaves and parsley, and garnish meat with onion rings. Makes 6 generous servings.

Tongue Marinade. Blend together 1 finely chopped sweet onion, ¾ cup olive oil, ½ cup white wine vinegar, ½ teaspoon salt, ¼ teaspoon pepper, and 1 teaspoon whole oregano.

Cooked Vegetables. Cook in the boiling reserved tongue broth, covered, 6 whole peeled carrots and 6 medium-sized peeled turnips just until each vegetable is barely tender. Remove vegetables from liquid with a slotted spoon and set aside.

Meanwhile, quarter 3 large peeled boiling potatoes and trim sections to resemble small whole potatoes. Then cook potatoes, covered, in boiling broth just until barely easy to pierce. Remove pan from heat and return carrots and turnips to liquid, adding 1/3 cup olive oil and 2 tablespoons vinegar. Chill, covered, overnight. If stock gels, warm slightly to release vegetables.

Simultaneously, cook separately, uncovered, in boiling salted water to cover, 3 or 4 medium-sized zucchini (each cut in half lengthwise), just until barely tender. Drain and chill quickly in ice water; drain well again. Moisten zucchini lightly with olive oil or salad oil and keep cold, covered.

Drain all vegetables before arranging with the meat.

Avocado Salads
ENSALADAS DE AGUACATES
(en-sah-*la*-thas de ah-gooah-*kah*-tehs)

The avocado sauce, Guacamole, used in so many dishes can also be served at least three ways as a salad.

For one version, you first put shredded or broken lettuce into a bowl and top it with a mound of Guacamole. Garnish with tomato wedges, olives, carrot sticks or curls, and radish roses. Sometimes this salad is served with a French dressing or mayonnaise.

Guacamole may also be spooned on top of tomato slices and served with a dressing if desired.

Another version is Aguacates Rellenos, or "stuffed avocados." As you make the Guacamole, scoop the pulp out carefully to leave the shells intact. Heap the seasoned, mashed avocado back into the shells and place them on lettuce leaves or shredded lettuce; garnish with lemon or lime wedges.

The recipe for Guacamole, including several variations, is on page 21. Crisp-fried tortilla chips (Tostadas), which you can make by instructions on page 30, or buy in bags, are always good accompaniment to the creamy salad.

COLD GAZPACHO, a soup containing chopped raw vegetables, can double as a salad (recipe on page 71).

Marinated Beef Salad
CARNE A LA VINAGRETA (vee-nah-*greh*-tah)

In many countries leftover cooked meat is made into a salad by cutting it into strips and marinating it in a vinaigrette sauce. The Mexican version is simple but has imaginative seasoning.

    4 cups cooked lean beef cut in strips
    1 large onion, thinly sliced
    2 tablespoons *each* capers and minced parsley
    ½ cup olive oil
    ¼ cup wine vinegar
    1 teaspoon crumbled oregano
    1 teaspoon prepared mustard
    ½ teaspoon salt

Put the meat strips on a rimmed platter and cover with the sliced onions. Sprinkle with the capers and parsley. Mix together the oil, vinegar, oregano, mustard, and salt. Pour over the meat, cover, and chill at least 3 hours to mingle flavors. Makes 6 servings.

VEGETABLES & RICE

Varied treatments of light and starchy accompaniments

Plain boiled vegetables, beans, or rice are about as uninteresting to Mexicans as a clay pot without colorful designs painted on it. To be considered edible, these foods must have something *done* to them.

Vegetables are not often served alone. Usually they are worked into other dishes for flavor, color, or texture. If cooked and served as nothing but a vegetable dish, they are embellished with sauce, cheese, meat, seasonings, or garnish. Sometimes several kinds of vegetables are combined.

The vegetables need not be highly spiced or seasoned. Sometimes they are just glorified with cream sauce, cream, or mild cheese, or flavored with onion. You probably could safely substitute many imaginative vegetable dishes from other countries in a Mexican meal.

Dried beans, rice, pasta, corn (either fresh or in hominy form), or other starchy foods used as accompaniments likewise are not allowed to reach the dinner plate unadorned.

Beans are faraway the most popular, with rice prepared in many "pilaf-type" ways following in second place. The sweet and white potatoes native to the country are eaten, but oddly they have never caught on to the extent that beans have. Perhaps this is all to the good of the national health, for beans and other legumes are rich in protein. For some reason, the potato has caught the fancy of people in more northern lands.

Refried Beans

Because Refried Beans are called for in so very many recipes in this book, instructions for making them appear in the basic sauces and fillings chapter on page 20. If you make your own beans, do not skimp on the hot bacon drippings, butter, or lard called for in order to cut calories; the secret of the best beans is ample use of fat. Canned beans can be improved by additional cooking with more flavorful fat.

The name "refried" should not be taken literally to mean "fried again." In Spanish the prefix "re" can mean merely "very" or "thoroughly." One frying is enough if it is a thorough one.

Stuffed Zucchini
CALABAZAS RELLENOS
(kah-lah-*bah*-sahs rrreh-*yeh*-nohs)

In Jalisco zucchini are stuffed with cream cheese and topped with sour cream. If you wish, fill the zucchini an hour or two ahead and then spoon the sour cream on just before baking.

    6 medium-sized zucchini
    1 package (3 oz.) cream cheese
    2 tablespoons minced onion
    ½ teaspoon salt
    ¼ teaspoon pepper
    1 cup (½ pint) sour cream
       Paprika (optional)

Place whole unpeeled zucchini in boiling water to cover; do not cover pan; reduce heat and simmer until nearly tender (approximately 10 minutes). Allow to cool until you are able to handle them, then cut each zucchini in half lengthwise and scoop out seeds into a small bowl. Mix the seeds with the cream cheese, minced onion, salt, and pepper.

Stuff this mixture back into the zucchini halves; arrange them in a buttered square baking dish or pan. Spoon the sour cream evenly over the top of each. Sprinkle with paprika, if you wish.

Bake for about 10 minutes in a 325° oven. Serve immediately. Serves 6.

Colache

(koh-*lah*-cheh)

Mexicans are undisputed experts on corn cookery, and this is one of the ways they use it fresh.

    2 tablespoons butter, margarine, or salad oil
    1 pound (about 4 small) zucchini or other
         summer squash, sliced
    1 small onion, chopped
    1 green bell pepper, seeded and diced
    ½ cup water
    1 large tomato, peeled, seeded, and diced
       About 1½ cups freshly cut corn
         (from 3 or 4 medium-sized ears)
       Water
       Salt and pepper to taste

Heat butter, margarine, or salad oil in a wide frying pan and stir in squash, onion, green pepper, and ¹/₂ cup water. Cover and cook over high heat, stirring frequently, for about 6 minutes.

Mix in tomato and corn. Cook, covered, for about 5 minutes more or until vegetables are all tender; stir occasionally. Add a little water if needed; season with salt and pepper. Serves 6 to 8.

Carrots in Milk

ZANAHORIAS EN LECHE

(sah-nah-*oh*-reeas en *leh*-cheh)

Carrots baked in milk with a garnish of minced parsley, Guadalajara-style, can dress up a family meal or lend balance to a menu of spicy dishes.

    8 large carrots, peeled and sliced very thin
    1 cup milk
    1 teaspoon sugar
    1 teaspoon salt
    ½ teaspoon pepper
    2 tablespoons butter or margarine
    2 tablespoons minced fresh parsley

Place carrots in a buttered 1¹/₂-quart casserole and cover with a mixture of the milk, sugar, salt, and pepper. Dot with butter and sprinkle parsley over the top.

Cover the casserole tightly and cook in a 350° oven for about 1 hour, or until the carrots are tender when pierced. Serve immediately. Makes about 6 servings.

Banana Fritters

CHURROS DE PLÁTANO

(*choo*-rrrohs deh *plah*-tah-noh)

Bananas are served as a vegetable with the simple roasted or broiled meats and fowl the Mexicans eat as frequently as they do the dishes known so well outside their country. They use fruit of a firm variety suited to cooking, dip them into lemon juice for tartness, and then into an egg batter which contains no sugar.

The bananas ordinarily sold in the United States can be used if they are green-tipped, not too ripe. Occasionally you will find fat, red-skinned cooking bananas (often called plantain) in some markets.

    3 firm, green-tipped bananas
       Lemon juice
    4 eggs, separated
    ¼ cup flour
    ½ teaspoon salt
       Salad oil, or part salad and part olive oil,
         for frying

Peel and split the bananas lengthwise; cut each piece in half. Dip in lemon juice.

For batter, beat egg yolks until thick and light. Add flour and salt. Beat the egg whites until stiff but not dry, and fold into yolks.

Drop the drained banana pieces into the batter, one at a time. Pick up with a spoon and slide into a large frying pan containing about 1 inch of hot oil. Cook over medium heat, turning almost at once; cook until brown on both sides. Drain on paper towels. Makes 6 servings.

Lemon Green Beans

JUDÍAS CON LIMÓN

(hoo-*thee*-as kohn lee-*mohn*)

Citrus juice often is the only touch that distinguishes that which is distinctly Mexican from what could be a dish from anywhere. In the Guadalajara area cooks prepare green beans with a simple parsley-butter sauce, then give it that typical finish—the juice of a fresh lemon.

    1½ pounds green beans, cut in 1½-inch lengths
            (or two 9-oz. packages frozen, cut
            green beans)
        Boiling salted water
     3 tablespoons melted butter or margarine
     ½ teaspoon salt
     ¼ teaspoon pepper
     1 tablespoon minced parsley
        Juice of 1 lemon

Cook beans uncovered in salted water to cover until tender-crisp. (Or cook as directed on the frozen green bean package.) Drain and place in serving dish. Pour a mixture of the butter, salt, pepper, parsley, and lemon juice over the top. Serve hot. Makes about 6 servings.

Eggplant Acapulco

BERENJENA A LA ACAPULCO (beh-ren-*heh*-nah)

Mushrooms and Romano cheese make this an out-of-the-ordinary eggplant dish. It's a good choice for a buffet dinner.

     1 large eggplant
        Boiling salted water
     ½ cup fine dry bread crumbs
     ½ cup grated Romano or Parmesan cheese
     ¼ cup (⅛ lb.) butter or margarine
        Salt and pepper to taste
     ½ pound fresh mushrooms, sliced
     2 cans (8 oz. *each*) tomato sauce

Place the whole, unpeeled eggplant in enough boiling salted water to cover completely; reduce heat and simmer for 10 minutes. Drain and allow to cool enough to handle. Cut it into quarters lengthwise; peel each quarter, then cut crosswise into 1-inch pieces; set aside. Mix the bread crumbs with the grated cheese.

Arrange layers as follows in a buttered 2-quart casserole, repeating layers once: eggplant pieces,

dots of butter, a sprinkling of salt and pepper, sliced uncooked mushrooms, tomato sauce, and the crumb-cheese mixture. Bake the casserole uncovered in a 350° oven for 30 minutes. Serve hot. Makes 6 servings.

Oaxacan Baked Black Beans

FRIJOLES NEGROS A LA OAXACA

(free-*hoh*-less *neh*-grohs ah lah ooa-*hah*-kah)

You'll need to plan ahead to make this dish from the south-coast state of Oaxaca—the small, black-skinned dried beans should bake about 10 hours. Substitute pinto beans if you can't find black ones. A few supermarkets, especially those stocking many gourmet foods, do have black beans. You might survey local markets by telephone if there is no Mexican store in your vicinity.

Party Brunch menu includes this dish (page 18).

     2 pounds dried black or pinto beans
    12 cups water
     2 cloves garlic, chopped
     1 medium-sized onion, chopped
    1½ teaspoons whole cumin seed
        About 2 pounds ham hocks (as lean as
            possible, or with some of the fat
            trimmed off)
     1 teaspoon salt
     ¼ teaspoon pepper
        Salt

Thoroughly wash and drain beans; place in a large casserole. Cover with water; add garlic, onion, cumin seed, ham hocks, 1 teaspoon salt, and pepper.

Cover and bake in a 275° oven for about 10 hours, or until beans are tender. (You can cook the beans overnight or start the day before, let stand overnight, and start again in the morning.)

Skim off as much fat as possible before serving, and add more salt if needed. Makes 8 to 12 generous servings.

Rice "Dry Soup"
SOPA SECA DE ARROZ (soh-pah seh-kah)

At fiesta or full-course meals, both a regular soup and a Sopa Seca or "dry soup" are included. This is dry in the sense that whatever liquid used during the cooking is completely absorbed into the filling foundation, usually something starchy such as rice, pasta, tortillas, or dried legumes.

This dry soup is the same thing as the tomato-flavored rice (sometimes called Spanish rice) you find served as a side dish along with the Refried Beans at most Mexican restaurants in the United States.

The variations on this basic dish which contain meat, seafood, or eggs can be entrées as well as accompaniments.

    2 cups uncooked rice
    6 tablespoons lard or shortening
    2 small onions, finely chopped
    2 cloves garlic, minced or mashed
    4 medium-sized tomatoes, peeled and chopped,
         or 1 cup tomato purée
    4 to 6 cups regular-strength beef or chicken broth
    2 or 3 canned California green chiles, or
         fresh green chiles, chopped (optional)
    2 tablespoons chopped parsley or chopped
         cilantro (also called Chinese parsley or
         fresh coriander), optional
    1 cup pimiento-stuffed green olives (optional)

Brown rice lightly in lard. Add onion, garlic, and tomato, and cook for 2 or 3 minutes; add 3 cups of stock and the chiles, if used.

Cover and simmer on top of range over medium heat for 25 to 35 minutes or bake in a covered casserole in a 350° oven 50 to 60 minutes. Add more stock or water if necessary to cook the rice. However, there should be no liquid remaining when the rice is done.

Adjust seasoning; add parsley or cilantro, if used, toward the end of the cooking period. Olives are for garnish. Makes 6 servings.

Rice Dry Soup with Shrimp. *(Sopa de Arroz con Camarón.)* Add 1 pound of cooked, shelled, deveined shrimp 5 minutes before rice will be done, to heat through. (Instead of stock, you can use the seasoned water in which you cooked the shrimp.)

Rice with Peas and Ham. *(Sopa de Arroz con Chicaros y Jamón.)* Add 1 pound diced cooked ham along with stock. About 10 minutes before rice is done, add 2 cups frozen peas, thawed.

Rice with Hearts of Palm. *(Arroz con Palmito.)* Add ¼ pound diced salt pork when browning the rice. Stir in 1 can (14 oz.) hearts of palm, drained and diced, about 5 minutes before rice is done, just to heat through.

Rice Soup with Eggs. *(Sopa de Arroz con Huevos.)* Make Sopa de Arroz, but 10 minutes before serving make six depressions in the top of the rice with the back of a tablespoon. Drop a raw egg in each, sprinkle with grated Parmesan cheese, and continue cooking until the eggs are set (covered on top of the range or in the oven).

White Rice
ARROZ BLANCO (ah-rrros blahn-koh)

Arroz Blanco is similar to rice pilafs you may already have made. Be sure to toast the rice slowly in the oil; this not only gives flavor but causes the rice to cook so that every grain is separate and fluffy.

Summer Buffet menu includes this dish (page 16).

    1½ cups uncooked long-grain rice
    ¼   cup salad oil
    1   clove garlic, whole
    1   medium-sized white onion, cut in half
    2   chicken bouillon cubes
    4   cups cold water
    ½   teaspoon salt

Place the rice in salad oil to which you have added the garlic clove and the onion halves. Slowly brown over low heat, stirring occasionally. When rice is wheat colored, pour off most of the oil (leave about 1 tablespoon) and remove garlic.

Crumble the bouillon cubes in the water, add salt, and pour over rice. Simmer, tightly covered, until liquid is absorbed, about 30 minutes. Serves 8.

BREADS, BOTH PLAIN & FANCIFUL

Some bland and others rich with sweet or spicy things

Tortillas are, of course, *the* bread of Mexico. They are also more than bread—an ingredient used in making many kinds of dishes.

Because the ways of preparing them and cooking with them are so varied, a whole chapter beginning on page 25 has been devoted to how to make them from scratch (or where to buy them), how to serve as simple bread accompaniment, and how to incorporate them in numerous dishes.

Both corn and flour tortillas are most frequently served as bread in a soft, steamy-hot form (often folded and wrapped in a napkin which helps keep them warm as long as possible). In the right-hand column of page 29, you will find instructions for reheating and softening tortillas—either those you make or those you buy.

Crisp-fried tortillas, whole ones or wedges, are another popular bread form. Frying instructions are in the left-hand column on page 30.

Additionally, other breads are also eaten. Some are plain wheat loaves or rolls, such as the *bolillo*, which is an oval, pointed, French-type roll. Other kinds of rolls have a bland flavor and porous texture or are puffy and flaky. These are formed into a myriad of fanciful shapes and given fanciful or funny names.

Some of the breads are sweet, perhaps studded with fruits and nuts. They may be good as a coffee cake or dessert, accompanied with Mexican hot chocolate.

Other kinds are deep-fried. Instead of crisp tortilla chips, you might like to make wheat-flour Sopaipillas, which come out of the hot fat puffy and crunchy (page 82).

Sweet Buns

PAN DULCE (pahn *dool*-seh)

The Mexicans often serve these round, flat sweet buns at *desayuno*, breakfast, or *merienda*, the late afternoon snack time.

>   1 package yeast, active dry or compressed
>   ¾ cup warm water (lukewarm for
>   compressed yeast)
>   3½ cups regular all-purpose flour
>   ¾ cup sugar
>   ½ teaspoon salt
>   3 tablespoons butter or margarine, melted
>   2 eggs, slightly beaten
>   Cinnamon-Flavored Topping (recipe
>   follows)

Dissolve the yeast in the ¾ cup water. Sift flour, measure, and sift again with the sugar and salt into a bowl. Add the yeast mixture, butter, and eggs; beat until smooth. Place dough in a greased bowl, cover, and let rise in a warm place until doubled in bulk, about 1½ hours.

Stir down, turn out onto a lightly floured board, and knead until smooth and elastic. Pinch off pieces of dough and shape into smooth, rounded balls about 1¼ inches in diameter. Place balls of dough on a greased baking sheet, about 2 inches apart. With the palm of your hand, press each ball down, flattening it slightly.

Gently spread about 1 tablespoon topping on each bun, and then let buns rise until doubled in bulk, about 30 minutes. Bake in a 400° oven for 10 minutes, or until lightly browned. Serve warm. Makes about 1½ dozen.

To freeze these buns, cool thoroughly, then wrap tightly. To reheat, place buns on a baking sheet in a 400° oven for about 3 to 5 minutes.

Cinnamon-Flavored Topping. Blend together 1 cup *each* sugar and sifted flour, ½ cup (¼ lb.) melted butter or margarine, 1 slightly beaten egg, 1 teaspoon cinnamon, and a dash of salt.

Three Kings' Bread

ROSCA DE LOS REYES
(*rrros*-kah theh lohs *rrreh*-yehs)

It is customary to serve *Rosca de los Reyes* ("Kings' Ring") to celebrate Twelfth Night, the 6th of January. The fruit-filled yeast bread is baked in a ring and garnished with "jewels" of candied fruits and nuts.

A tiny doll or lima bean is hidden inside the bread. The guest who receives the wedge with the doll is obliged to give another party on the coming February 2, a religious holiday called *El Dia de la Candelaria.*

Twelfth Night Party menu includes this dish (see page 17).

2 packages yeast, active dry or compressed
1 cup warm water (lukewarm for compressed
   yeast)
5 cups unsifted regular all-purpose flour
¼ cup instant non-fat dry milk
1 cup (½ lb.) soft butter or margarine
½ cup sugar
1 teaspoon salt
3 eggs
   Butter
½ cup *each* raisins and chopped walnuts
¼ cup chopped candied cherries
1 tablespoon *each* grated orange and
   lemon peel
3 tablespoons light or whipping cream
2 cups sifted powdered sugar
½ teaspoon vanilla
   Candied fruits and nuts for garnish

Dissolve yeast in warm water. Add 1¼ cups unsifted flour and the dry milk; beat well with a wooden spoon—2 to 3 minutes. Cover and leave in a warm place about 30 minutes.

Meanwhile, in a separate bowl, cream the butter or margarine with the sugar and salt. Beat in the eggs, one at a time; add to first mixture;

beat again about 3 minutes. Gradually stir in 3¾ cups unsifted flour.

Turn out dough on a lightly floured board and knead until smooth and elastic (about 8 minutes); place in a buttered bowl. Turn once to bring the buttered side up; cover and allow to rise in a warm place until nearly doubled in bulk, about 1½ hours.

Combine raisins, walnuts, candied cherries, orange and lemon peel. Pat dough out to about a 10-inch round on a floured board, top with the fruit-nut mixture, and fold up edges of dough and knead in the fruit and nuts until evenly distributed.

Divide dough in half; form each half into a long roll (about 20 inches); join ends of each roll to form the rings and place each on a greased baking sheet. Cover and allow to rise about 30 minutes. Bake in a 400° oven for 25 to 30 minutes. Cool baked loaves; cut out a small triangle from the top of one and insert a tiny doll (see note following); replace wedge.

Glaze with a mixture of the cream, powdered sugar, and vanilla. Decorate with "jewels" of candied fruits and nuts, left whole or sliced attractively. Makes 2 ring-shaped loaves.

Note. In Mexico a tiny china doll is usually baked right in the loaf. However, you may have trouble finding a china doll small enough and have to settle for a plastic one which would, of course, melt during the baking. Therefore the preceding method of inserting the doll is recommended. The sugar glaze will completely disguise where you have hidden it.

A lima bean may be baked in the loaf, but it could be hazardous to the teeth of whoever might bite into it. The doll is a safer choice.

Puffy Fried Bread

SOPAIPILLAS (soh-paee-*pee*-yas)

This puffy, crisp, deep-fried bread makes a pleasant change from tortillas to accompany many types of dishes.

Winter Buffet menu includes this dish (see page 18).

    4 cups regular all-purpose flour
1¼ teaspoons salt
    3 teaspoons baking powder
    3 tablespoons sugar
    2 tablespoons shortening
       Milk (about 1¼ cups)
       Salad oil for deep frying

Sift flour, measure, and sift again with the salt, baking powder, and sugar. Cut in the shortening, and add milk to make a soft dough just firm enough to roll. Cover bowl and let dough stand for 30 to 60 minutes; then roll ¼ inch thick on lightly floured board and cut in diamond-shaped pieces.

Heat about 1 inch of oil in a frying pan to about 370° to 380°. Add a few pieces at a time; turn at once so they will puff evenly, then turn back to brown both sides. Drain on paper toweling. Serve with butter. Makes 4 dozen or more.

"Pants" Biscuits

CALZONES (kahl-*soh*-nehs)

This rolled dough makes a bland sweet biscuit, much like the popular American sugar cooky, which is cut into the shape of a pair of men's pants. *See photo on opposite page.*

½ cup plus 2 tablespoons shortening
    7 tablespoons sugar
    4 cups regular all-purpose flour
    5 teaspoons baking powder
    1 teaspoon salt
1¼ cups milk
¼ cup sugar
¼ teaspoon cinnamon

Cream shortening and the 7 tablespoons sugar until fluffy. Sift flour, measure, then sift again with baking powder and salt. Gradually add dry ingredients to the creamed mixture alternately with milk, mixing until blended. Roll out the dough on a lightly floured board to ¼-inch thickness.

To shape each biscuit: With a sharp-pointed knife, cut out a piece of dough with a base 1¾ inches wide, sides 2¼ inches high, and top 1½ inches wide. Cut a small V-shaped wedge from the middle of the base and a smaller V-shaped wedge from the middle of the top. (A paper pattern made before you begin speeds the cutting. See photograph on opposite page for sample of baked biscuits.)

Place biscuits on a greased baking sheet slightly apart. Sprinkle with a mixture of the sugar and cinnamon. Bake in a 350° oven for 15 to 20 minutes, or until light brown. Makes about 4½ dozen.

Corn Pie

PASTEL DE ELOTE (pas-*tehl* del-*loh*-teh)

Pastel de Elote, which means "corn pie," is made of fresh corn in Mexico, but canned cream-style golden corn makes a marvelous all-season substitute. The bread may be made ahead and reheated.

    1 cup (½ lb.) butter or margarine
    1 cup sugar
    4 eggs
    1 can (4 oz.) California green chiles,
       seeded and chopped
    1 can (1 lb.) cream-style golden bantam corn
½ cup shredded jack cheese
½ cup shredded mild Cheddar cheese
    1 cup regular all-purpose flour
    1 cup yellow cornmeal
    4 teaspoons baking powder
¼ teaspoon salt

Preheat oven to 350°. Cream butter and sugar. Add eggs, one at a time, mixing in well. Add chiles, corn, and cheese; mix well.

Sift flour and then measure; sift cornmeal and then measure; sift both together with baking powder and salt and add to corn mixture, blending well. Pour into greased and floured baking dish (8 by 12 by 2 inches). Put dish in oven and reduce heat to 300°. Bake for one hour. Serves 10.

Puff Paste Rolls

HOJALDRE (oh-*hal*-dreh)

Many paper-thin layers of flaky pastry, or *hojal-dre*, are the basis for two rolls, in "book" and "bow-tie" shapes. Like standard puff pastry, this pastry is rolled out, spread with butter, and folded many times to incorporate the butter between the layers.

Be sure to roll the pastry very thin ($1/8$ or $3/16$ inch thick) before cutting the pastry in pieces. The pastry puffs tremendously while baking and will not hold its shape if too thick.

    4   cups regular all-purpose flour
    ¼   teaspoon cream of tartar
    ½   teaspoon salt
    1½ cups (¾ lb.) soft butter or margarine
    1   tablespoon lime or lemon juice
    1   cup ice-cold water
    ¼   cup sugar
    ¼   teaspoon cinnamon
    ¼   cup finely crushed sugar cubes

Sift flour, measure, then sift again with cream of tartar and salt. Cut in 1 cup of the butter until the butter is the size of large peas. Add lime or lemon juice. Gradually add the cold water, a few tablespoons at a time, stirring with a fork until the dry ingredients are dampened. Knead several times only, just enough to blend, on a lightly floured board.

Roll out pastry $1/4$ inch thick in a large rectangle. Dot the pastry with 2 tablespoons of the softened butter and spread the butter over the surface as evenly as possible. Starting from the left side, fold over $1/3$ of the pastry; fold the right $1/3$ of the pastry over the other $1/3$ of the pastry, making 3 layers. Roll lengthwise into a long rectangle; spread with another 2 tablespoons of the butter. Fold $1/3$ of the pastry up from the bottom; fold top $1/3$ of the pastry down so it covers the other $1/3$. Turn folded pastry so it faces you vertically.

Roll, butter, fold, and turn pastry 4 times altogether. Place on baking sheet, cover with waxed paper, and chill thoroughly.

Let puff pastry stand at room temperature for 45 minutes. Cut in halves. Then shape half into book and the other half into bow-tie-shaped rolls according to following instructions.

Book (Libro) Rolls. Roll into a rectangle $1/8$ inch thick and cut into long strips $1½$ inches wide.

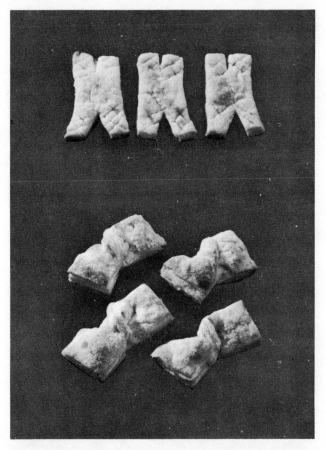

SHAPED BREADS delight Mexicans; among the many kinds are "Pants" Biscuits (top) and "Bow Tie" Puff Paste Rolls.

Then cut the strips crosswise in $2½$-inch pieces. Fold each piece of dough crosswise in half to make a "book." Place on an ungreased baking sheet. Sprinkle with a mixture of sugar and cinnamon and then with the crushed sugar cubes.

Bake in a 400° oven for 20 to 25 minutes, or until golden brown. Remove from baking sheet to cool. Makes 4 dozen "books."

Bow Tie (Corbata) Rolls. Roll into a rectangle $3/16$ inch thick and cut into strips 1 inch wide. Then cut the strips crosswise into 3-inch pieces. Pick up each piece of dough with both hands and twist it in the center, making a half twist. Place on an ungreased baking sheet. Sprinkle with a mixture of the sugar and cinnamon and then the crushed sugar cubes.

Bake in a 400° oven for 20 to 25 minutes, or until golden brown. Remove from baking sheet to cool. Makes 40 "bow ties." *See photograph above.*

DESSERTS & SWEETS

Delights to end a meal or satisfy a sweet tooth anytime

Luscious puddings and custards, many further enriched with egg, are the most characteristic desserts of an already rich cuisine. These are made with a number of seasonings and ingredients. The flavoring may be cinnamon, almond, caramel, fruit, or cheese. Bread or even corn may be used for the more robust versions.

The variety of such sweets is attributed to the Spanish nuns, who vied among themselves to produce interesting new treats for special occasions, religious holidays, or to honor visiting dignitaries. Some of the classic dishes, sweet and otherwise, originated this way.

Even today, Mexican nuns are noted for their elaborate desserts and confections, some of which are sold to raise funds for church or charities.

Other typical desserts are pastries, such as Buñuelos, pancake-thin, deep-fried puffs. Or turnovers called Empanadas, which may be filled with a variety of sweet mixtures.

Fruits, particularly the tropical types, and coconut often appear in desserts and confections.

You may always end a meal with fresh fruit or melon (with lime wedges if appropriate).

Before the Spaniards introduced flour, sugar, and milk products, the ancient Mexicans probably had few foods to satisfy sweet tooths, other than fresh fruit and honey. But they did make berry-stuffed versions of Tamales. Now Tamales are prepared not only with a variety of fruits but also with a caramel filling of dark brown sugar and sometimes nuts.

These unusual specialties would probably be the most surprising treat you could offer to people who think Mexican food means Chile con Carne and "Hottamales." Sweet Tamales make a marvelous late afternoon or evening snack, particularly with a cup of Mexican hot chocolate. They also are delicious for breakfast. The recipes for fruit and caramel Tamales are on page 48.

Dessert Turnovers

EMPANADAS (em-pah-*nah*-thas)

Mexicans make their pastry turnovers called Empanadas with both sweet and meat-type fillings. Here are three delicious sweet fillings for dessert Empanadas.

If you prefer, substitute pie-crust mix (enough for a double-crust pie) for the following pastry recipe.

Summer Buffet menu (page 16) and Midnight Christmas Eve Supper menu (page 19) include this dish.

2 cups regular all-purpose flour
½ teaspoon salt
⅔ cup shortening
4 tablespoons cold water
    Filling (recipes follow for 3 types)
    Butter (optional)
    Sugar and cinnamon (optional)

Sift flour, measure, and sift with salt into bowl. Cut shortening into flour with pastry blender until pieces are about the size of large peas. Sprinkle water by tablespoonfuls over the top of mixture and toss dough with a fork to moisten evenly. Turn out on waxed paper, press dough into a ball, and wrap it in the paper. Chill.

Roll out chilled dough ⅛ inch thick and cut into 4 or 5-inch circles (or 3-inch circles for miniature turnovers, Empanaditas). Spoon filling on one side of each circle. Dampen edges of dough, fold over, and press edges together with fork. Brush with butter if you wish.

Bake in a 400° oven for about 20 minutes, or until browned. If you wish, roll the hot Empanadas in sugar mixed with a little cinnamon. Makes 12 to 15 Empanadas, or about 3 dozen Empanaditas.

Filling recipes are on next page.

Pumpkin-Raisin Filling. Combine in a pan 1 cup canned pumpkin, ¼ cup sugar, ½ cup raisins, 2 teaspoons anise seed, and ¼ teaspoon salt. Bring to a boil and simmer for 10 minutes; cool before using.

Sweet Potato-Pineapple Filling. Combine 1 cup cooked and mashed sweet potatoes with ½ cup chopped blanched almonds, 1 cup (9 oz. can) drained crushed pineapple, ½ teaspoon salt, and 1 tablespoon sugar. If you like a sweeter filling, add more sugar—the Mexican cook would probably do so.

Cheese-Currant Filling. Mash 1 cup country-style cottage cheese with the back of a spoon; blend in 1 very-well-beaten egg, ½ cup sugar, ¼ teaspoon *each* salt and cinnamon. Mix in ½ cup dried currants and ¼ cup golden raisins.

Bread Pudding

CAPIROTADA (kah-pee-roh-*tah*-thah)

This dessert has many variations, but all contain cheese and fruit. It's a good way to use up the last of a loaf of French bread.

¾ cup brown sugar, firmly packed
½ teaspoon cinnamon
¾ cup water
2½ cups French bread cubes
    (cut ½-inch-square)
¾ to 1 cup raisins (seeded raisins, seedless
    raisins, currants, or a combination)
¾ cup chopped walnuts
½ cup diced sharp Cheddar cheese
2 teaspoons butter
    Sweetened whipped cream or
    ice cream (optional)

In a pan combine brown sugar, cinnamon, and water; boil gently until sugar is dissolved. Pour the hot syrup over bread cubes and toss gently. Add the raisins or currants, walnuts, and cheese; toss again until blended. Spoon into a 1½-quart casserole or baking pan, greased with the 2 teaspoons butter.

At this point you can let the pudding stand until about 20 minutes before you plan to serve it. Bake in a 375° oven for about 15 minutes, or until heated through. Serve warm, with whipped cream or ice cream if you wish. Makes about 6 servings.

Baked Pineapple, Natillas

PIÑA AL HORNO CON NATILLAS
(*pee*-nya *lor*-no kohn nah-*tee*-yass)

Hot baked pineapple served from its leafy pineapple shell is topped with a chilled custard sauce.

Winter Buffet menu includes this (page 18).

1 large or 2 medium-sized fresh pineapples
    About ¼ cup sugar
2 or 3 tablespoons rum or 1 teaspoon
    rum flavoring
¼ cup (⅛ lb.) butter
    Natillas Sauce (recipe follows)

Lay pineapple on its side and take off a thick slice (off one side) that does not include the green top. Carefully scoop out the insides and cut into bite-sized pieces. (Or if you prefer, stand the pineapple up and cut off its top to remove the insides.)

Sweeten the pieces to taste with about ¼ cup sugar. Flavor with rum or rum flavoring. Put pineapple pieces back into pineapple shell. Dot the top with the butter, cover with foil (including the green leaves), and bake in a 350° oven for 20 minutes. Replace the top and bring it to the table on a plate to serve warm, topped with the cold sauce. Serves 8 to 12.

Natillas Sauce. Scald 1 pint half-and-half (light cream); cool slightly. Add ¼ teaspoon salt, ¼ cup sugar beaten with 1 whole egg and 2 egg yolks, 1 teaspoon cornstarch, and 1 teaspoon vanilla. Cook over hot water, stirring constantly, until smooth and slightly thickened. Chill.

CHEESE PUDDING (Chongos) preparation begins with slicing a rennet-milk pudding into neat, uniform squares.

PUDDING SQUARES, slowly heated 6 hours, shrink and become firm; they look and taste much like cream cheese.

Cheese Pudding in Syrup

CHONGOS ZAMORANOS

(*chohn*-gos sah-moh-*rah*-nos)

This unusual pudding was the discovery of some long-forgotten cook in Zamora, a city famed for dessert specialties, in the state of Michoacán southeast of Lake Chapala. Chongos (meaning "little knots") are tender, sweet, white lumps with a faint caramel flavor and cheese-like consistency. (In fact, the technique for preparing them greatly resembles that for making cottage cheese.) First you prepare a milk-rennet pudding, then cut the set mixture into pieces and cook very slowly over lowest heat.

The *photographs above* show you how to cut the pudding into squares once it has set. A little care in cutting will produce much more attractive results. Divide the surface into even squares, using a ruler. With a thin, sharp knife, gently cut straight downward (be careful not to mar the bottom of the pan with the point of the knife).

You have to cook Chongos about 6 hours, but they require absolutely no attention, except to check the rate of cooking. Then you transfer the Chongos to a spicy syrup; this makes them firmer and adds flavor.

You have a choice of ingredients to use in the syrup. For a deliciously rich caramel taste and straw color, use the Chongos cooking liquid; for a clear spiced syrup, use water as the base.

2 quarts homogenized milk
4 rennet tablets, finely crushed
4 tablespoons cold water
¾ cup sugar
3 teaspoons vanilla
**2 cinnamon sticks, each 3 inches long,
      broken into smaller lengths**
1 cup sugar
2 cups water or Chongos liquid

Heat the milk until it feels lukewarm (110°). Mix rennet with the 4 tablespoons water, the ¾ cup sugar, and vanilla, and stir thoroughly into the milk in the pan. Let stand undisturbed at room temperature for 1 hour or until set.

Note: If the milk does not set, it has been heated to the wrong temperature, either too hot or not hot enough. You may reheat the milk, adding 4 more rennet tablets, if setting does not occur the first time.

CHONGOS SQUARES soak in a light syrup delicately spiced with cinnamon. Sticks of the cinnamon used to flavor the syrup make an attractive garnish. This pudding can be made days ahead of time.

With a knife divide the surface into 1 to 2-inch squares (smaller pieces make firmer Chongos; larger pieces are softer in texture); cut straight down through the mixture to pan bottom (see photographs above).

Set pan on lowest heat and cook, uncovered, for 6 hours; the mixture should never get hot enough to cause motion in the pan as this will break up the squares. *Do not stir.* After 6 hours the Chongos should be white and as firm as warm cream cheese.

Combine the cinnamon and the 1 cup sugar with the 2 cups water or Chongos liquid (drain or siphon out the 2 cups with a bulb baster, disturbing the Chongos as little as possible, then pour liquid through a cloth to remove scraps; add water if necessary to make the 2 cups liquid). Bring to a boil in a deep pan; boil 5 minutes.

Gently transfer Chongos in a slotted spoon to the hot syrup. Let stand until lukewarm before serving, or chill. (To store, cover and refrigerate up to 2 weeks.) To serve, spoon several Chongos and some of the syrup into each bowl. Makes 5 to 6 servings.

Photo above shows Chongos in syrup.

Mango Cream

CREMA DE MANGO (*kreh*-mah theh *mahn*-goh)

Easily prepared but festive in appearance, this sweet fruit dessert offers interesting contrasts of texture.

Fresh mangoes are ripe when slightly soft (about the same "feel" as a ripe avocado or papaya).

Dinner for Guests menu includes this page 16).

5 large ripe mangoes, or 2 cans
    (14 oz. *each*) mangoes
    Sugar
2 oranges, peeled, seeded, and cut in
    small pieces
1 tablespoon lemon juice
1 pint (2 cups) heavy cream, whipped
1 cup broken pecans
12 *each* green and red maraschino cherries

Peel and sieve mangoes and add sugar to taste (the Mexicans like it sweet). Add oranges, lemon juice, and whipped cream. Fold in pecan meats and serve in parfait glasses. Top each with a green and a red cherry. Serves 12.

Almond Pudding

ALMENDRADO (al-men-*drah*-thoh)

Almendrado, in Spanish, means "almond-like"; it is also the very appropriate name of an almond-flavored pudding. Part of the meringue is white and the balance is tinted pink and green (you can color or not, as you like).

- 1 envelope unflavored gelatin
- ¼ cup cold water
- 5 egg whites
- ¾ cup sugar
- ½ teaspoon almond extract
- ¼ teaspoon grated lemon peel
  Red and green food coloring
  Almond Custard Sauce (directions follow)

Soften gelatin in cold water, then dissolve over hot water. Add to the egg whites in the large bowl of an electric mixer. Beat whites at highest speed until they form a thick, white foam. Continue beating and add the sugar 1 tablespoon at a time, gradually sprinkling in each spoonful over a period of 1 minute. When whites hold soft, curving peaks as the beaters are withdrawn, add the almond extract and lemon peel and beat in thoroughly.

Tint ⅓ of the meringue a pale pink with a few drops of red food color, and tint another ⅓ of the meringue a pale green with a few drops of green food color. Pile the pink, white, and green meringue mixtures side by side in a shallow bowl and chill at least 2 hours or as long as about 6 hours. With a cap of foil, cover the meringue without touching it (it is easily marred).

Spoon the meringue into dessert bowls and pour Almond Custard Sauce over each serving. Makes 6 servings.

Almond Custard Sauce. In the top of a double boiler blend thoroughly 5 egg yolks, ¼ cup sugar, 2 cups milk, and ¼ teaspoon grated lemon peel. Cook, stirring constantly, over gently simmering water until mixture thickens enough to coat the back of a metal spoon in a velvety layer. (If there is any sign of graininess at any time, remove custard from heat at once and set in cold water, stirring to cool quickly.)

Add ¼ teaspoon almond extract and ¾ cup toasted slivered almonds to the custard, then set pan in cold water and stir to cool. Cover and chill (as long as overnight).

Milk Pudding

LECHE QUEMADA (*leh*-cheh keh-*mah*-tha)

Dulce de Leche, which means "milk sweet," and Leche Quemada, or "burnt milk," are both names for this dessert. The second name may refer to what can—but shouldn't—happen when the dessert is being cooked for as long as 6 hours, until thick and caramel-colored. Or the word "burnt" may refer to the caramel quality, as caramel is sometimes called burnt sugar.

The dessert is so rich that you should serve it in tiny containers, such as cordial glasses, nut cups, or Oriental teacups.

- 1 quart milk
- 2 cups sugar
- 1 teaspoon vanilla or drop of
    almond extract (optional)
  Chopped nuts (optional)

In a heavy pan over high heat, bring the milk and sugar to a full boil. (For a darker, more caramel-like *dulce*, substitute ¼ cup brown sugar for an equal amount of white sugar.) Immediately reduce heat to low, and cook; the mixture should bubble gently.

When it takes on a caramel color and thickens to the consistency of a caramel topping or light pudding (this will take 5 to 6 hours), remove from the heat and cool. Flavor with vanilla or almond extract, if you wish.

Set in the freezer or refrigerator to chill; in the freezer it becomes a little firmer. (Dulce de Leche keeps a week in the refrigerator or freezer.) If you like, top with chopped nuts. Serves 8; about 3 tablespoons are sufficient for one serving.

Caramel Custard

FLAN (flahn)

Egg custard, baked in its own caramel sauce, is a classic sweet served all over Europe and the Middle East, even in many other parts of the world wherever the cuisine has Continental influence. In both Spain and Mexico the custard is known as Flan. At Mexican restaurants in the United States, Flan is the dessert most often available.

⅓ cup sugar
6 eggs
6 tablespoons sugar
2 cups milk
1 teaspoon vanilla

To make hot water bath for the Flan, set a 9 by 1¼-inch pie pan in a slightly larger pan. Fill the outer pan with just enough hot tap water to come up around the other pan; hold down the pie pan so it won't float. Then remove the pie pan and put only the pan of water in a preheating 350° oven while you mix the custard.

In a small frying pan over moderate heat melt the ⅓ cup sugar; shake pan instead of stirring. Once melted, the sugar will caramelize quickly; as soon as it does, pour at once into the 9-inch pie pan. Using hot pads to protect hands, tilt pan quickly to let syrup flow over bottom and slightly up sides. If syrup hardens before you finish, set pan on moderate heat until syrup softens, then continue.

Beat together to blend the eggs and 6 tablespoons sugar; add milk and vanilla. Set caramel-lined pan in hot water in oven; pour in the egg mixture. Bake in a 350° oven for about 25 minutes; test by gently pushing custard in center with back of a spoon—when done a crevice about ⅜ inch deep forms.

Remove from hot water and chill at once. As the Flan cools, the caramel dissolves somewhat. When cold, loosen just the custard edge, then cover with a rimmed serving plate. Holding plate in place, quickly invert. The Flan will slowly slip free and the caramel sauce flow out. To serve, cut in wedges, spoon on sauce. Serves 6.

Fresh Prickly Pear Dessert

POSTRE DE TUNAS (pos-tre theh too-nas)

Prickly pear is the general term for the edible fruits of certain cactus. The fruits are also called Indian figs or cactus pears; the Mexican word is tunas (not to be confused with nopales, cactus leaves which are also edible). Beneath the treacherous, thorny skin of the prickly pear is sweet pulp which can make an intriguing dessert that is easy to prepare.

If you live in a warm, dry climate, you may have a prickly pear plant in your own yard. If not, look for the fruits in your produce market or a Mexican grocery in the fall until mid-December.

Although other cactus produce edible fruits, those most commonly used are from the large plants with big pad-like joints, known as Opuntia. The fruits are oval and range from apricot-size to 5 inches long and 3 inches across. Some are yellow-green, rose-red, or purple-black. Considered choicest for eating are the large, rich rosy red fruits of an 8 to 12-foot-high cactus (O. Megacantha) native to Mexico.

The prickly pears you'll find in the market are usually pretty well denuded of their reddish brown, bristly spines. But to pick them from a cactus plant requires special care. Wear heavy leather gloves, or use several thicknesses of paper toweling or newspaper to grasp the fruit, then cut it off with a long knife.

To prepare the fruit in the kitchen, hold with tongs and rinse under cold running water. Lay on a plate or cutting board, still holding with tongs or a fork. Cut off both ends of the fruit, slit the skin lengthwise, loosen and lay it back. Lift out the pulp.

Flavors of the various prickly pears differ somewhat, but all have a pleasing, fruity quality when ripe. They're delicious eaten as they are, as a fresh fruit.

For a simple dessert, slice large pieces of the fruit pulp into a sherbet glass, sweeten if desired, top with sweetened whipped cream, stick a lime wedge onto the glass rim, and squeeze the juice on as you eat.

BUÑUELOS (Fried Sweet Puffs) can be glazed with a brown sugar syrup or sprinkled with white sugar and cinnamon.

Fresh Corn Pudding

PUDÍN DE ELOTE (poo-*theen* del-*loh*-teh)

Mexicans use corn in a variety of ways, even desserts. This pudding of fresh corn and eggs puffs like a soufflé and falls just as quickly.

    1 cup fresh corn kernels (about 2 or 3 ears)
    3 eggs, separated
    ½ cup sugar
    1 teaspoon cinnamon
    ½ teaspoon vanilla
    ⅛ teaspoon salt
       Sweetened whipped cream or
          vanilla ice cream (optional)

Whirl corn in a blender with egg yolks (or grind through fine blade of a food chopper, then beat in yolks). Mix in sugar, cinnamon, vanilla, and salt. Beat egg whites until they hold short, distinct peaks. Fold in the yolk mixture thoroughly. Pour into a buttered 1-quart dish.

Bake in a 375° oven for 25 to 30 minutes or until top feels quite firm when tapped lightly. Serve immediately. Unauthentic toppings are whipped cream or ice cream. Serves 4 or 5.

Fried Sweet Puffs

BUÑUELOS (boo-*nyue*-los)

In Mexico these crisp pastries are sugar-glazed and eaten as a mid-afternoon sweet.

In Oaxaca, they are also featured in a curious celebration. All year long vendors save cracked or irregular pottery. On Christmas Eve they gather in the city square and sell Buñuelos, served on the pottery. Customers eat the pastries on the spot, then break the dishes much as people in other countries delight in smashing wine glasses on special occasions. By midnight the square is heaped with broken crockery.

The photograph in the left-hand column shows Buñuelos with both sugar and glazed coatings.

Twelfth Night Party menu includes this dish (see page 17).

    3⅓ cups regular all-purpose flour
      1 teaspoon salt
      1 teaspoon baking powder
    1½ tablespoons sugar
      ¼ cup (⅛ lb.) butter or margarine
      2 eggs
      ½ cup milk
         Salad oil for deep frying
         Sugar or glazed coatings
            (see following instructions)

Sift flour, measure, then sift again with salt, baking powder, and sugar into a bowl. Add butter and rub into flour with your fingertips until mixture is like coarse meal. Beat eggs lightly with milk, then pour into flour mixture and stir until dough forms a solid mass. Turn dough out onto board, and knead lightly for 2 minutes or until smooth. Cut dough into balls the size of marbles and let stand 15 minutes.

Roll each ball on a lightly floured board into a very thin pancake 4 inches in diameter. Cut a hole in center with a thimble. After you roll out the circles of dough, place them in a single layer on waxed paper until you are ready to cook.

Fry in hot deep fat (375°) until puffed and golden brown, about 30 seconds on each side. Drain on paper towels. Use one or both of the following coatings. Makes 6 dozen.

Sugar-Coated Buñuelos. Mix 1 cup granulated sugar and 1 teaspoon cinnamon in a paper bag. Reheat Buñuelos in a 250° oven for 5 minutes, then shake gently, one at a time, in bag to coat with sugar-cinnamon mixture.

Glazed Buñuelos. Place ½ cup *each* granulated sugar, light brown sugar (firmly packed), and water in a frying pan. Add 1 tablespoon butter or margarine, 1 teaspoon cinnamon, and 1 tablespoon dark corn syrup. Heat, stirring, until sugar melts, then boil rapidly for 1 to 2 minutes, or until two drops of syrup run together off spoon. The glaze will still be a thin syrup.

Remove from heat and cool for 1 minute; then place Buñuelos in pan, one at a time, and spoon over syrup until coated on both sides. Drain on wire rack for 30 minutes. The coating will be slightly tacky, but not drippy. Makes enough to glaze about 20 Buñuelos.

Coconut Candy

DULCES DE COCO (*dool*-ses deh *koh*-koh)

This white fondant candy often is tinted bright green or a deep pink. These colors may seem a strange choice until you consider that they are to Mexicans what red, white, and blue are to Americans—flag colors.

1 coconut
   Water
4 cups sugar
   Food coloring (optional)

Make holes in the eyes of the coconut and drain liquid into a cup. Crack coconut; taste meat to be sure it is free from off-tastes. Remove brown husk and finely shred meat to make 2 cups.

Add enough water to the coconut liquid to make 2 cups. Place water mixture and sugar in a saucepan, and cook over highest heat, stirring until mixture is clear. Wash syrup spatter from pan sides with a brush dipped in water. Put candy thermometer in syrup and continue to cook, without stirring, at highest heat until temperature is 238°; wash pan sides once or twice with wet brush.

At 240° immediately remove pan from heat, wash pan sides again, and quickly place thermometer where syrup is to be poured. Pour syrup onto marble slab or into a ceramic tray or platter that is at least 10 by 12 inches, making sure to cover the tip of the thermometer; *do not scrape the pan.*

Let stand undisturbed until cooled to at least 110° or no colder than 90° (if thermometer is not in syrup, get an accurate reading by tipping it or turning it face down to immerse mercury bulb, then check). Avoid movement in syrup as much as possible, or it may become grainy.

Stir cooled syrup with a metal spatula or wooden paddle, agitating it quickly and continuously until it turns opaque, white, and thickens to a firm, plastic mass that does not readily adhere to your fingers when lightly touched (usually 10 to 15 minutes). Work mass with your hands in a kneading motion until it is glistening and smooth.

Place kneaded candy in the top part of a double boiler; melt over hot water, stirring occasionally, until it is the consistency of heavy cream. Stirring as little as possible, add the shredded coconut and enough food coloring to tint mixture the desired color. Or divide the melted candy and leave one part white; tint the second part bright green and the third part pink. Drop by teaspoonfuls onto waxed paper; cool until hardened. Makes 9 dozen candies.

Orange Candy

DULCES DE NARANJA (nah-*rahn*-hah)

This candy has the same creamy consistency as fudge, and you use about the same techniques for making it.

3 cups sugar
¼ cup water
1 cup undiluted evaporated milk
   Pinch of salt
2 teaspoons freshly grated orange peel
1 cup chopped walnuts

Put 1 cup of the sugar into a heavy frying pan and stir with a wooden spoon over medium heat until the sugar is melted and caramelized to a golden brown color. Add the water and stir until the sugar completely redissolves. Add the remaining 2 cups sugar, evaporated milk, and salt.

Place over low heat and stir until the mixture begins to boil. Cook, stirring frequently, until it reaches the soft ball stage (236°).

Remove from heat; cool to lukewarm, without stirring. Add the orange peel and nuts. Beat until the candy loses its gloss and will hold its shape when dropped from a spoon. Pour into a lightly buttered 8-inch-square pan and cool until set. Cut into squares before candy becomes too firm.

HOT & COOLING DRINKS

Tangy potables worthy of festive or simple celebration

South of the border that old familiar airline beverage question should be—¡*Café, té, o chocolate?* The milk you will likely get either in the coffee or in the hot chocolate.

Coffee often is made like French *Café au Lait* and similarly called *Café con Leche*. Hot milk is mixed in equal proportion with hot coffee made about four times as strong as American coffee. Coffee with milk is drunk not only at breakfast but later in the day as desired and with meals.

For after-dinner service, coffee brewed at about the same strength as that made in the United States will be sweetened and spiced with stick cinnamon and whole cloves. The sugar used usually is *piloncillo*, sometimes called *panocha*, which is sold in little cone-shaped cakes. American dark brown sugar is an adequate substitute.

Rivaling coffee with milk in popularity, hot chocolate beaten to a foamy "head" may also be served at various hours of the day, particularly *desayuno* (breakfast) and *merienda* (the late-afternoon snack or light-supper time). Instructions for chocolate are on the next page.

Tea may be infused from the customary Indian and Oriental tea leaves but more likely from a variety of herbs, dried flowers, and barks. The hot herbal teas, or *tisanes*, are reputed to cure a vast array of ailments from toothache to shattered nerves.

Some intriguing cold drinks are made from dried flowers or barks, others from ground seeds or nuts. Flowers called *jamaica*, which look like wrinkled black mushrooms in their dried state, literally blossom when soaked in cold water from four hours to overnight. The resulting infusion is a beautiful cranberry pink. You strain off the clear liquid, sweeten it to taste, and serve icy cold, preferably on the hottest of days. Jamaica can be purchased in Mexican groceries in the United States.

Fruit-ades and juices are drunk by young and old. *Turistas* are always surprised by the quantities of freshly squeezed orange juice available. Plain juices and fruit punches make very appropriate beverages with all Mexican meals.

Coconut-Lime Drinks

BEBIDAS DE COCO Y LIMÓN
(beh-*bee*-thas deh *koh*-koh ee lee-*mohn*)

The delicious coconut milk drinks with lime and tropical fruit juices served in Mexico are a surprise to some tourists who think of such concoctions as Polynesian only.

     2   cups coconut milk
     ½   cup fresh lime juice
          Canned guava, papaya, *or* passion fruit juice
          Sugar
          Rum (optional)

If you use frozen coconut milk, thaw it and whirl in a blender before mixing the drinks.

To make milk from packaged coconut, combine 2²/₃ cups *each* flaked coconut and cold milk; refrigerate 1 hour. Whirl in a blender for about 40 seconds. Strain through a double thickness of cheesecloth, squeezing out 2 cups milk.

To make fresh milk, drain and crack 1 coconut; taste to make sure it is free from any off flavors. Cut meat in ½-inch cubes. For each cup of cubed meat, add ³/₄ cup hot liquid (hot water added to the liquid from the coconut). Whirl in a blender for 20 to 30 seconds, then steep 30 minutes. Strain through a double thickness of cheesecloth, squeezing out about 2 cups milk.

With the 2 cups coconut milk and ½ cup fresh lime juice, you can make the following drinks by adding the specified amounts of juice, sugar, and rum. Serve each over ice immediately after mixing. *(Continued on next page.)*

Coconut-Guava. Combine the coconut milk and lime juice with 6 cups (four 12-oz. cans) guava nectar, ³/₄ cup sugar, and 1 cup rum. Makes 8 drinks.

Coconut-Papaya. Combine the coconut milk and lime juice with 2 cups (one 12-oz. can contains 1¹/₂ cups) papaya juice, ¹/₂ cup sugar, and ¹/₂ cup rum. Makes 4 drinks.

Coconut-Passion Fruit. Combine the coconut milk and lime juice with 3 cups (two 12-oz. cans) passion fruit nectar, ¹/₂ cup sugar, and ¹/₂ cup rum. Makes 4 drinks.

Hot Chocolate
CHOCOLATE (choh-koh-*lah*-teh)

Mexican hot chocolate, a popular beverage much more frequently served than the similar thing in the United States, is best made with rich milk, flavored with cinnamon, and beaten until frothy. You can easily make the proper drink with squares of unsweetened chocolate, powdered spice, and an electric or hand beater.

But for authenticity and the sheer fun of it, you may want to buy imported chocolate and a typical wooden chocolate beater. The chocolate is sold in cakes or pellets already containing the necessary sugar and cinnamon, and usually almonds and egg. The almonds are for flavor, and the egg to produce more froth. These cakes are sold in bulk, or in packages labelled "Mexican confection," which fail to mention the purpose and therefore often are mistakenly placed on grocery shelves along with candy.

The primitive chocolate beater is a decoratively carved instrument which resembles a bass drum stick, with grooves and loose wooden rings just above the knobby end to produce the froth. You put the end with knob and rings in the hot chocolate and hold the other slender end between your palms. Rub your palms together to twirl the beater—the way Indians once twirled a stick in a stone to strike sparks for starting a fire. (Former Boy and Girl Scouts will already have the technique down pat.)

The beater, called a *molinillo,* was designed by ancient Mexican Indians and still is used, even in many a modern kitchen. You may find moli-

nillos in some import shops, as well as Mexican stores. Because they look so much like a toy, they, too, may be displayed in an unlikely section of the store.

For each 2 servings, use half of a 2-ounce cake of prepared Mexican chocolate (or a 1-oz. square of unsweetened chocolate, 1 tablespoon sugar, a pinch of salt, and ¹/₂ teaspoon cinnamon). Combine with 2 cups of milk and cook over hot water until the chocolate melts. Beat until foamy and pour into cups; or pour into a pitcher and beat with the molinillo where your guests can watch.

Tropical Fruit Punch
PONCHE TROPICAL (*pon*-cheh troh-pee-*kal*)

This typical punch contains four fruits much enjoyed south of the border—pineapple, orange, papaya, and guava. The flavor harmonizes with many dishes and soothes spicy ones.

Summer Buffet menu includes this (page 16).

    4 to 8 slices fresh peeled pineapple
    2 small oranges, peeled
    4 to 8 slices fresh peeled and seeded papaya
 1½ cups orange juice
    2 cans (12 oz. *each*) guava nectar
    4 mint springs

Arrange in *each* of 4 large glasses 1 or 2 slices of the pineapple; ¹/₂ an orange, sliced; and 1 or 2 slices of the papaya.

Fill glasses with a mixture of the orange juice and guava nectar. Chill and serve garnished with mint sprigs. Sip juice with a straw and eat fruit with a spoon. Makes 4 servings.

SANGRÍA, punch of orange juice and red wine, is cooling at any time and refreshing served with spicy foods.

Orange Sangría

SANGRÍA DE NARANJA
(sahn-*gree*-ah theh nah-*ran*-hah)

Sangría, a red wine punch of Spanish origin, is served throughout Mexico, with or without food. Some versions contain lemon or lime juice, but this particular kind with orange alone is one of the smoothest and most praiseworthy yet devised. *(See photograph above.)*

Dinner for Guests menu includes this drink (see page 16).

    1 medium-sized orange
    ¼ cup sugar
    2 cups freshly squeezed orange juice
    1 bottle (4/5 qt.) dry red wine
    ½ cup Cointreau (or other orange-flavored
        liqueur)

Cut the orange in half. Cut 1 or 2 thin slices from one half, cut them into quarters, and save for garnish. With a vegetable peeler, thinly cut off the thin outer peel of the other half of the orange. In a bowl, using a spoon, bruise the peel with the sugar to release the flavorful oils; then stir in the orange juice, wine, and orange-flavored liqueur. Cover and chill; after the first 15 minutes, remove the orange peel.

Serve Sangría in a bowl or from a pitcher, garnished with the quartered orange slices. Add ice cubes to the individual servings, if you like. Makes 6 cups, or 12 servings of ½ cup each.

Lime Sangría Float

SANGRÍA DE GUADALAJARA (gooah-tha-la-*hah*-rah)

In Guadalajara they make a Sangría of red wine floating on a lime-flavored sparkling water base. Straws are inserted in the glass, and you may use them to sip from each layer or swirl to blend.

Winter Buffet menu includes this drink (see page 18).

For Each Serving:
    Simple Syrup (recipe follows)
    1½ tablespoons lime juice
    ⅓ cup chilled sparkling water *or* club soda
        Ice cubes
    ½ cup chilled dry red wine

In a glass that will hold at least 1½ cups, blend 2 tablespoons Simple Syrup, lime juice, and chilled sparkling water. Drop in 4 or 5 ice cubes, then *carefully* pour chilled dry red wine onto ice; the wine will float in a distinct layer on the sparkling-water base.

Insert drinking straws and serve. Makes 1 serving.

Simple Syrup. Combine ½ cup *each* sugar and water in a saucepan and bring to a boil, stirring; cook until clear. Chill thoroughly. Makes almost ⅔ cup, enough for 5 drinks.

Index